A CRITICAL GUIDE
to the
SEND CODE OF PRACTICE
0–25 Years (2015)

A CRITICAL GUIDE
to the
SEND CODE OF PRACTICE
0–25 Years (2015)

Janet Goepel, Jackie Scruton and Caroline Wheatley

First published in 2020 by Critical Publishing Ltd

British Library Cataloguing in Publication Data
A CIP record for this book is available from the British Library

ISBN: 978-1-913063-33-7

This book is also available in the following ebook formats:
MOBI ISBN: 978-1-913063-34-4
EPUB ISBN: 978-1-913063-35-1
Adobe ebook ISBN: 978-1-913063-36-8

Cover design by Out of House Limited
Text design by Greensplash
Project Management by Newgen Publishing UK
Printed and bound by 4edge Limited, UK

Critical Publishing
3 Connaught Road
St Albans AL3 5RX

www.criticalpublishing.com

Paper from responsible sources

Contents

Acknowledgements

The authors would like to thank Bridget Graham, Ursula Holdsworth, Dr Ben Ko (consultant paediatrician and governance lead for the British Academy of Childhood Disability) and Dr Paul Wright (council member of the British Association for Community Child Health). Their patience in reading drafts and giving us very helpful feedback has enabled us to further understand the role of different practitioners who are involved in supporting children and young people with special educational needs (SEN). We would also like to thank Professor Kevin Forsyth (Professor of Paediatrics and Child Health, Flinders University, Adelaide) for his encouragement and professional support.

Janet would like to thank her fellow authors Jackie and Caroline for stimulating and enlightening professional discussions, as well as the enjoyment of good food and company over our writing weekends. Janet's husband John and daughters Sarah and Rachel have all been supportive and encouraging, as well as providing light relief at times during the writing process. Her thanks to them.

Jackie would like to say thank you to both Janet and Caroline for their friendship and support. She will miss those conference calls! Her husband John has had to listen to endless conversations, especially as the political climate has changed during the project. For this she thanks him and promises her writing career is over.

Caroline would like to thank Janet and Jackie for welcoming her to the world of academic writing. The process of creating this book has been instrumental in further shaping her belief in the importance of early identification and intervention for children and young people with SEN. Many thanks go to her family for their support.

Meet the authors

Janet Goepel

I have been a teacher for many years, working with a range of children with the label of SEN. I moved to working in higher education teaching inclusion and SEN after completing my master's. My doctoral thesis is concerned with the professionalism of doctors and teachers in working together to support children with SEN. Working as a SEN co-ordinator (SENCO) in a school, I was all too aware of the importance of good interprofessional working as well as relationships with parents and the children and young people themselves. I have presented papers on this theme in the UK and in Australia to teachers and health professionals. I am currently a senior lecturer in primary education at Sheffield Hallam University and teach inclusion and SEN on the undergraduate and postgraduate initial teacher training courses. I am the leader for the PGCE award in SEN Co-ordination and also National Priority Lead for Special Educational Needs and Disability (SEND) for all primary and early years teacher education courses within Sheffield Hallam University. This enables me to continue to work with professionals and those in training to help bring about better outcomes and life chances for children and young people.

Jackie Scruton

I started my work with children and young people with SEN at the age of 15 when I undertook work experience in a local special school. I soon realised that this was the path for me. I qualified as an NNEB nursery nurse and spent the next 14 years working in a variety of settings, from a residential boarding school for boys with emotional and behavioural difficulties to an inner-city family centre, a special school and further education colleges. I went on to gain a degree as a mature part-time student, quickly followed by an MA in SEN. This broadened my eyes to the wider issues of SEN, in particular inclusion, and led me to teach in higher education and to become a specialist member of the Special Educational Needs and Disability Tribunal (SENDIST).

Caroline Wheatley

I taught for many years within the primary age phase, becoming a SENCO and subsequently training as a specialist teacher in dyslexia and literacy. I managed a local authority learning support service and until recently was service leader for a group of seven inclusion services that together address all four of the main areas of SEND. This role enabled me to see the graduated response to need at all levels in action on a daily basis, from the perspectives of children, young people and their families, as well as from colleagues in education, health and social care.

Acronyms used in this book

ADHD	attention deficit hyperactivity disorder	DCSF	Department for Children, Schools and Families
AET	Autism Education Trust	DDA	Disability Discrimination Act
BACCH	British Association for Community, Child Health	DfE	Department for Education
BACD	British Academy of Childhood Disability	DfES	Department for Education and Skills
CAMHS	Child and Adolescent Mental Health Service	DH	Department of Health
CCG	clinical commissioning group	DHSC	Department of Health and Social Care
CDC	Council for Disabled Children	DISS	Deployment and Impact of Support Staff
CEAS	Children's Education Advisory Service	DM	Designated Medical Officer
CLDD	complex learning difficulties and disabilities	DSA	Disabled Students' Allowance
CnYP	children and young people	DT	designated teacher
		EAL	English as an additional language
CoP	Code of Practice	EDTA	Effective Deployment of Teaching Assistants
CP	Care Plan	EEF	Education Endowment Foundation
CPD	continuing professional development	EFA	Education Funding Agency
CQC	Care Quality Commission		
CSDPA	Chronically Sick and Disabled Persons Act	EHC	education, health and care
CYPn	child or young person	EP	educational psychologist
DCO	Designated Clinical Officer	EYFS	Early Years Foundation Stage
		FE	further education

GDPR	General Data Protection Regulation	POET	Personal Outcomes Evaluation Tool
GP	general practitioner	PP	Pathway Plan
HAP	health action plans	P scale	Performance scale
HCP	health care plan	SALT	speech and language therapist
HP	health practitioner		
INMSS	independent and non-maintained special schools	SCE	Service Children's Education
		SCP	social care practitioner
JSNA	Joint Strategic Needs Assessment	SEN	special educational needs
LA	local authority	SENCO	special educational needs co-ordinator
LDD	learning difficulties and/or disabilities		
		SEND	special educational needs and disability
LEA	local education authority		
LGO	Local Government Ombudsman	SENDIASS	SEND Information, Advice and Support Service
LO	Local Offer		
MAT	multi-academy trust	SENDIST	Special Educational Needs and Disability Tribunal
MOD	Ministry of Defence		
NC	national curriculum	SLD	severe learning difficulties
NHS	National Health Service		
NNPCF	National Network of Parent Carer Forums	SMART	specific, measurable, achievable, realistic, time-bound
Ofsted	Office for Standards in Education, Children's Services and Skills		
		SpLD	specific learning difficulties
OT	occupational therapist	SPP	Service Pupils' Premium
PA	personal adviser	TA	teaching assistant
PCFs	parent carer forums	TAC	Team Around the Child
PCP	person-centred planning	TAF	Team Around the Family
PEP	personal education plan	WSOA	written statement of action
PHSO	Parliamentary and Health Service Ombudsman		
		YOT	youth offending team
PMLD	profound and multiple learning difficulties	YP	young people
		YPn	young person

Legislation and guidance

Being aware of legislation and guidance that underpins and informs practice is crucial for all practitioners. This is listed here in ascending date of publication order. The table indicates to which services the legislation has particular relevance. Additionally, the SEND Code of Practice itself provides you with details of relevant regulations at the start of each chapter.

Act/guidance	Purpose	Applicable to which agency?		
		Education	Health	Social care
The Chronically Sick and Disabled Person Act 1970	Requires local authorities to provide welfare services for people with disabilities			✓
Children Act 1989	Comprehensive framework for the care and protection of children Up to age 18 years		✓	✓
Education Act 1996	Post-Warnock Report sets out the framework for inclusive education	✓		
Inclusive schooling (DfES, 2001)	Provides statutory guidance on the practical operation of the statutory framework for inclusion	✓		
Children Act 2004	To improve children's services with a focus on early intervention, a multi-agency approach and safeguarding issues	✓	✓	✓

Act/guidance	Purpose	Applicable to which agency?		
		Education	Health	Social care
National Health Service Act 2006	Consolidated previous legislation, sets out the structure of the health service and aims to promote physical and mental health		✓	
Mental Capacity Act Code of Practice (2007)	Guidance for decisions made under the Mental Capacity Act 2005, supporting care and treatment of over 18-year-olds who lack capacity	✓	✓	✓
Apprenticeship, Skills, Children and Learning Act 2009	Makes provision for apprenticeships and training	✓		
Equality Act 2010	Protects individuals from discrimination, harassment and victimisation	✓	✓	✓
Health and Social Care Act 2012	First Act to cover health inequalities. Emphasises the importance of physical and mental health		✓	
Ensuring a good education for children who cannot attend school because of health needs (DfE, 2013)	Statutory guidance for local authorities	✓		✓
Care Act 2014	Local authorities have a duty to assess and provide support for publicly funded care needs			✓
Children and Families Act 2014	Part three covers children and young people with SEND	✓	✓	✓

Act/guidance	Purpose	Applicable to which agency?		
		Education	Health	Social care
Special Educational Needs and Disability Code of Practice: 0 to 25 years (DfE and DH, 2015) (first published 2014)	Statutory guidance for organisations which work with and support children and young people who have special education needs or disabilities	✓	✓	✓
Supporting Pupils at School with Medical Conditions (DfE, 2015)	Statutory guidance from the Department for Education about the support that pupils with medical conditions should receive at school	✓	✓	
Statutory Framework for the Early Years Foundation Stage (DfE, 2017d)	This framework details a set of standards that all early years providers must meet	✓		
Quick Guide: Guidance for health services for children and young people with SEND (NHS England, 2018a)	Guidance for joint commissioning of services for children and young people with health care needs		✓	
Quick Guide: Commissioning for transition to adult services for young people with SEND (NHS England, 2018b)	Guidance for implementing joint commissioning		✓	
Working Together to Safeguard Children (DfE, 2018c)	Statutory guidance for inter-agency working to safeguard and promote the welfare of children	✓	✓	✓

Introduction to the book

How to read the book

The Warnock Report in 1978 (Department of Education and Science, 1978) was a landmark in the world of education and in SEND in particular. Since then, successive governments have introduced new legislation with new supporting policies and guidance. These initiatives have had fundamental implications for children and young people (CnYP) as well as their parents and those working within education, health and social care. In the Foreword for the *Special Educational Needs and Disability Code of Practice: 0 to 25 Years* (SEND CoP) the government states that its vision for

> *children with special educational needs and disabilities is the same for all children and young people – that they achieve well in their early years, at schools, and in college, and lead happy and fulfilled lives.*
>
> (DfE and DH, 2015, p 11)

While this is a laudable aim, the outworking of this in practice is more problematic. Hodkinson (2016, p ix) acknowledges the difficulties of understanding and making sense of notions such as SEN, inclusion and disability. He recognises that this is a '*world where professionals, families and administrators coexist with each other*' and that there are '*competing agendas*' to manage while seeking to meet the needs of CnYP.

Hodkinson (2016) also identifies that while those working with CnYP are expected to carry out the requirements of the SEND CoP, the forming and development of such practices are determined by '*government departments, education and health policies, civil servants and the public at large*'. Such bodies provide the '*political will that confirms, conforms and constrains*' SEN policy and practice and contributes towards what Tomlinson (2012) terms the '*SEN industry*'. Therefore, while this book does provide guidance on how to interpret and enact the CoP, it also raises questions and exposes dilemmas. The guidance for the CoP takes an approach which considers the child or young person (CYPn) according to age through different phases of education and beyond. However, we have chosen to take an approach which considers the CYPn from early identification of need, regardless of age, to the possible requirement of an education, health and care (EHC) plan. It deliberately focuses on CnYP and their parents and considers their experiences and journey as they seek to navigate their way through the complications of systems, processes and working practices of different organisations and services.

Critical thinking and implications for practice

While this book is written with CnYP firmly in mind, we also consider the contributions that different practitioners make in enabling CnYP with SEN or disability to achieve their aspirations as the CoP expects. It is all too easy for practitioners to operate in silos and to fail to understand the difficulties this might pose for other practitioners and especially for CnYP and their parents. The aim of this book is to help you to understand the roles and responsibilities of all agencies and practitioners involved in this area of work. It is written to enable you to identify complexity and dilemmas, to understand perspectives that may be different from your own and to provide you with theoretical frameworks that enable critical thinking.

Similarly, this book provides an opportunity for all practitioners to reflect on their own practice and to use their deeper understanding of the requirements of the CoP as well as a consideration of the perspectives of others, in order to inform their own practice further. As Bolton (2010, p 13) states 'Length of experience does not necessarily confer insight and wisdom. Ten years of experience can be one year's worth of distracted experience repeated ten times'. Therefore, a continual reflexive position is vital for all those working with CnYP with SEN or disability.

As CnYP develop and change, so the way their needs are met is also subject to change. The critical thinking questions and implications for practice features within each chapter of this book provide an opportunity to take stock and to reconsider values and beliefs. An integration of these values and beliefs, along with the expectations set out in the CoP, will encourage flexible and authentic approaches to best meet the needs of CnYP who need additional provision.

Getting the best out of the book

It is important that you have an understanding of the meaning of certain terms and conventions used in the book. We have chosen to use the term 'special educational needs' (SEN) rather than 'special educational needs and disability'. This is because the Children and Families Act (2014, clause 20) uses the term SEN to refer to CnYP who have learning difficulties and/or disabilities (LDD) which mean they have greater difficulty in learning than children of the same age or in accessing facilities provided for their peers. The term SEN therefore carries with it the weight of legislation. It is clause 77 of this Act which gives rise to the CoP which is the subject of this book. However, where the term SEND has been used in reports or research, we have been faithful to the language the document has used.

The guidance provided in the CoP is statutory and to emphasise this the CoP has written the word '**must**' in bold. In order to be consistent, we have adopted the same convention.

The SEND CoP provides statutory guidance relating to Part 3 of the Children and Families Act 2014 and was originally published in July 2014. However, a revised CoP was published in January 2015. In order to ensure the most up-to-date information is utilised, we refer to the 2015 revision of the CoP throughout this book.

We recognise that there can be confusion concerning how those who work with CnYP are referred to. Those working within education, health or social care services are often referred to as professionals. This can suggest a hierarchy between such people and the parents of the CnYP. In order to recognise the expertise that parents have regarding their children and to acknowledge them as equal partners, we have chosen to use the word practitioner to refer to all parties. Additionally, wherever the term parent occurs throughout the book, this is intended to embrace carers and all those with parental responsibilities for CnYP.

It is also worth noting that within this book we have referenced the SEND CoP, paragraphs 7.37 and 7.38. However, within the CoP itself, these paragraphs do not appear at the end of Chapter 7 as you might expect, but within Chapter 8, p 122, as part of the introduction to that chapter.

The structure of the book

The book is divided into three parts, each of which considers an important element of information and practice relating to the 2015 SEND CoP. These are:

Part one   Introduction to the SEND Code of Practice 0–25 Years

Part two   Knowing the Child or Young Person;

Part three   Education, Health and Care Plans.

Each of the chapters within these three parts provides an overview of the content of the chapter followed by an explanation of the aspect of the CoP being discussed. The information given concerning the CoP is further examined using wider theory and models, such as models of partnership and disability. Where appropriate, the process of making provision for CnYP with SEN is detailed along with the roles and responsibilities of the different practitioners involved. Each chapter provides further reading on aspects of the themes discussed in the chapter as well as relevant web-based materials. In this way, you should gain deeper knowledge and understanding of the CoP and its wider political and social context as well as how this has relevance to CnYP with SEN and those who work with them. Being aware of legislation and guidance that underpins and informs practice is crucial for all practitioners. This information is provided separately in a table, which can be found at the front of the book.

Part one: introduction to the SEND CoP

Part one enables you to develop your understanding of the context of the SEND CoP (DfE and DH, 2015). Chapter 1 includes an examination of the historical and legal background to SEN, together with an exploration of discourses around SEN, such as the use of labels. Practitioners working together is a key aspect of the current CoP and Chapter 2 examines who these practitioners are and how they are involved in ensuring joint outcomes for CnYP. The focus for this joint working is across education, health and social care services. We detail key duties: **must**, should and could (DfE and DH, 2015, p 12). **Must** is a key statutory duty and as such has to be provided; should is what should be provided as part of the support package; could is the expectation of what could be provided within current resources. Finally, Chapter 3 explores what is meant by the Local Offer.

Part two: knowing the child or young person

Part two of this book focuses on the need to get to know the CYPn in order to ensure that appropriate holistic provision and support is put in place. The first step in this process is to ensure that proper assessments are carried out at every age and phase of the CYPn's life journey. This part of the book explores the importance of gaining the views of CnYP as central to any decision-making processes with regard to their future aspirations. It is important to understand that once a CYPn's SEN have been assessed and identified, relevant provision should be put in place. This is delivered via three approaches to provision: universal, targeted and bespoke. Each of these approaches is discussed in more detail in Part two as follows:

- Chapter 4 – universal provision;
- Chapter 5 – targeted provision;
- Chapter 6 – bespoke provision.

In each of these chapters we consider how the 'assess, plan, do, review' cycle or graduated response should be implemented. In this part of the book we also examine how different agencies have a role to play, especially in providing information for the LO.

Part three: education, health and care plans

Part three begins by illustrating in Chapter 7 the basic process and principles relating to an EHC assessment which may result in an EHC plan. Chapter 8 addresses this process from a parent's and CYPn's perspective in more detail and considers how young people with SEN should be supported in preparing for adulthood. This includes how transitions from one education setting to another should be managed as well as the implications of transitioning into employment. Chapters 9, 10 and 11 specifically address the perspectives of education, health and social care practitioners in making effective provision for CnYP with SEN and for whom an EHC plan may be considered. Chapter 12 considers the requirements of implementing an EHC plan while in Chapter 13, the final chapter, we outline the review process, including reasons for an early review and for ceasing to maintain an EHC plan.

PART ONE INTRODUCTION TO THE SEND CODE OF PRACTICE

1 Understanding the context

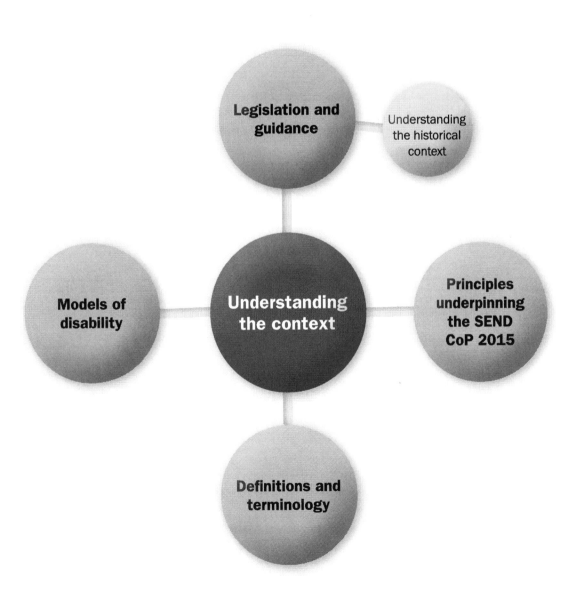

Legislation and guidance

Understanding the historical context

Models of disability

Understanding the context

Principles underpinning the SEND CoP 2015

Definitions and terminology

This chapter provides:

- an understanding of the framework for the SEND CoP within the context of past legislation and guidance;
- identification of the principles underpinning the 2015 SEND CoP;
- a consideration of definitions and terminology within the field of SEND;
- a discussion of medical and social models of disability.

Legislation and guidance

The 2015 SEND CoP makes reference to other relevant legislation, which can be seen in the table at the beginning of this book. It is important to note that while much of the legislation shown originates from, and is relevant to, education, this is not exclusively the case. Some of the legislation has particular relevance to health and social care services.

Understanding the historical context

The Mental Deficiency Act 1913 identified four categories or labels of mental deficiency:

1. idiots;
2. imbeciles;
3. feeble minded;
4. moral imbeciles.

This terminology is rooted in medical/psychological diagnosis. The impact of such a label on the individual might have meant the difference between living at home or being placed in an institution. This was a period in which CnYP were considered to require medical intervention or support and in which a deficit model was at the forefront.

The Education Act 1944 continued to use labels to categorise CnYP. The Act introduced 11 new categories of disability, together with a new generic category *educationally sub normal* of which there was a secondary *severely* label. These CnYP did not have a right to education and fell under the responsibility of the local health authority.

The Warnock Report (Department of Education and Science, 1978) was influential in the passing of the 1981 Education Act. This report introduced the term *special educational needs* and represented a shift towards a more inclusive system of education especially given that it stressed the importance of professionals working with parents as partners. The subsequent Education Act 1981 adopted much of the philosophy of the Warnock Report. The key aspect of the Act was the introduction of a *Statement of SEN*, a legally binding document outlining the needs of a CYPn and the provision required to meet those needs. A further Education Act 1993 resulted in the introduction and implementation of the SEN CoP (DfE, 1994). This code was revised (DfE, 2001) following the Education Act 1996.

With each change of government came new legislation and a revision of the CoP. The most recent revision, which is the subject of this guide, was in 2015 after the introduction of the Children and Families Act 2014.

Other milestones during the development of education for CnYP with SEN include the Disability Discrimination Act (DDA) 1995, and the Special Educational Needs and Disability Act 2001, which enshrined in legislation the fundamental right of a CYPn with a Statement of SEN to be educated in a mainstream school, albeit with some caveats. Additionally, the 2009 Lamb Report (Department for Children, Schools and Families, 2009), based on detailed research, underpinned the need to strengthen parental voice and confidence to help improve the quality of partnership working.

The Children and Families Act 2014 replaced the Statement of SEN with an EHC plan and subsequently a new SEND CoP was introduced, with a further revision in 2015 (DfE and DH, 2015). This requires teachers to make high quality provision through a differentiated approach and following the four-part cycle of assess, plan, do and review. We examine this in more detail in Part two.

More recently, the House of Commons Education Committee has published a report with a focus on how the SEN system works. It recognised that the Children and Families Act 2014 originally set out the ambition to transform SEN provision and put CnYP at the heart of that transformation. These transformations were seen as positive; however, this report identifies that the current political environment has meant that these reforms have not been fully realised. Factors influencing this are poor administration, a challenging funding environment and lack of ability in local authorities (LAs) and schools in understanding and carrying out the reforms. The report also recognised that there is a tension between the needs of CnYP, the provision available and a lack of accountability. However, it confirms what many CnYP and their parents are experiencing. '*This generation is being let down – the reforms have not done enough to join the dots, to bring people together and to create opportunities for all young people to thrive in adulthood*' (House of Commons, 2019a, p 4).

Principles underpinning the SEND CoP 2015

The principles that underline the legislation in terms of education, health and social care are as follows.

- CnYP and their parents are involved in discussions and decisions about their support.

- CnYP and their parents are involved in planning and commissioning services.

- The needs of CnYP are identified early and early intervention is given.

- CnYP and their parents have greater choice and control.

- There is greater collaboration between education, health and social care services.

- There is high quality provision.

- There is a focus on inclusive practice and removing barriers to learning.

- Support is provided to make a successful transition to adulthood.

These principles are examined in more detail in Parts two and three of this book.

Definitions and terminology

This section aims to enable you to develop a wider understanding of the complexities of terminology and definitions within SEN, as these are often different depending on which practitioner you are talking to – it is the dilemma of defining difference.

The notion of SEN has been subject over the years to a changing environment in language and categorisation. Mittler (2000, p 9) suggests that 'SEN terminology has survived for so long because it is not easy to find an acceptable substitute … it is embodied in legalisation'.

In examining the CoP, while there is a clear legal definition, the terminology could still be said to label, with words such as *special educational needs* or *greater difficulty in learning*. Interestingly, the only reference to labelling issues is seen in the 1994 CoP and not the most recent version (Lehane, 2017), yet the practice of labelling children is rife within education, health and social care.

In regard to legislation for social care, a child with a disability by default is defined as a child *in need* (Children Act, 1989). It is important to understand that the use of a range of definitions/terminology can cause difficulty for all practitioners including parents.

However, even with different definitions, we are constrained by the legal definitions in the SEND CoP and these are used throughout this book, namely:

> *A child or young person has SEN if they have a learning difficulty or disability which calls for special educational provision to made for him or her.*
>
> (DfE and DH, 2015, p 15)

and

> *A child of compulsory school age or a young person has a learning difficulty or disability if he or she:*
>
> - *has a significantly greater difficulty in learning than the majority of others of the same age, or*
>
> - *has a disability which prevents or hinders him or her from making use of facilities of a kind generally provided for others of the same age in mainstream schools or other post-16 institutions.*
>
> (DfE and DH, 2015, p 16)

Table 1.1 *Some of the terminology used across sectors*

SEN	Special educational needs	Education – schools
SEND	Special educational needs and disability	Education – schools
LDD	Learning difficulties and/or disabilities	Post-16 – FE, health and social care contexts
AEN	Additional educational needs	Education – schools
ASN	Additional support needs	Education – schools
	Children in need	Children's services
	Disabled children	Children's services and children's health services
ALN	Additional learning needs	Education – schools

The definition for disability as stated by the DDA (1995, 50 1 (1)) uses language that might be better suited in a medical context. It defines disability as: '*A physical or mental impairment which has a substantial and long-term adverse effect on a person's ability to carry out normal day-to-day activities.*'

The use of terminology within the field of SEN can be complex and confusing, as each sector has its own language. See Table 1.1 for some examples.

SCENARIO

You are a practitioner (from education, health or social care) who has been asked to meet the parents of a young person (YPn) aged 17 who has a diagnosis of Asperger's. You have been given a number of reports and letters from all the agencies involved who are working with the YPn. These include the local further education (FE) college, the social worker and the community paediatrician. These reports use a large number of acronyms and terminology you are not familiar with and as a result you are struggling to get a clear picture of the YPn.

CRITICAL QUESTIONS

- How might you find out what the acronyms all mean?
- In your role, what can you do to ensure there is consistency and continuity of terminology?
- What could you do to ensure the YPn and their parents understand each organisation's terminology, how it relates to them and what this means for the support they offer?

As already identified, different terms can be used to describe a CYPn. Many of these stem from the framework each profession uses within that particular context. These frameworks can be influenced by different models of disability. These are explored in the next section along with implications for practice.

Models of disability

Within the field of SEN there are a number of theoretical frameworks or models that are used. In order to understand your role as part of a multi-agency team you need to have an understanding of these frameworks and how they might have influence on practice.

The traditional and perhaps commonly used model is known as the medical model, which focuses on a CYPn's impairment; on what they cannot do rather than what they can do. It can be viewed as a deficit approach. There is a focus on *'cure'* and *'rehabilitation'* (Frederickson and Cline, 2015, p 11) in which treatments and strategies can cure or ameliorate the disability (Hodkinson and Vickerman, 2012), using normal functioning as a bench mark. Within the CoP, phrases such as *'majority of others of the same age'* and *'making use of facilities of a kind generally provided for others of the same age'* (DfE and DH, 2015, p 16) are used. Both implicitly infer difference from what is considered to be the norm. No external factors such as environment are taken into account (Frederickson and Cline, 2015; Garner, 2009). The medical model is best summed up by listening to the voice of the disabled:

> *It has kept people focused on our difficulties and deficits so it is easy to think we are useless, burdensome and dispensable.*
>
> (Mason, 2008, p 33)

The social model of disability arose from the disability rights movement during the 1970s and 1980s (Oliver, 2000) and takes a more inclusive approach. It suggests the *fault* lies with society; it is society that places barriers in the way and in doing so hinders and prevents participation in wider society. It is not the CYPn's impairment that is the barrier, rather society's difficulty in accommodating difference (Frederickson and Cline, 2015).

Both models are not without their critics; the medical model does not consider the social characteristics of disability, while the social model may be deemed to over-socialise the causes of disability (Terzi, 2005). It should be noted that nowhere in the CoP, in any of its iterations, is there an explicit mention of models of disability, yet the language seems driven by the medical model with the use of vocabulary such as '*additional to*' (DfE and DH, 2015, 6.15) and '*disorders*' (DfE and DH, 2015, 6.32). While only two models are examined in this chapter, there are others such as the charity and affirmative models. You can find out more about these through the links in the further reading section at the end of this chapter.

CRITICAL QUESTIONS

Think about your personal role in supporting CnYP with SEN and use this as the basis for reflecting on the following critical questions.

- What language do you use when you are describing a CYPn? Does it reflect one of the models of disability we have discussed?

- Does your use of language label in either a constructive or a negative way? How do you know?

- How does your service define SEN and disability? Does it follow any of the models we have discussed? Is the approach used one that is enabling or disabling?

- How might you effect change in your organisation to ensure CnYP are seen as individuals and are not defined by their label?

IMPLICATIONS FOR PRACTICE

With reference to your own profession or role in supporting CnYP with SEN:

- identify which legislation is pertinent to that role;

- explain how you would ensure you comply with the legislation.

Conclusion

Having knowledge about the legal and historical background to SEN is an important part of understanding the current context for your professional practice. Chapter 2 develops this theme and explores working together for joint outcomes.

Further reading and web-based materials

Models of disability: the following two websites provide a clear explanation of these models.

The affirmative model: disabilityarts.online/magazine/opinion/towards-affirmative-model-disability/ (accessed 31 July 2019).

The charity model: www.emeraldinsight.com/doi/abs/10.1016/S1479-3547(01)80018-X (accessed 31 July 2019).

A good starting point for exploring and understanding SEN, including how to support CnYP in practice, is:

Wearmouth, J (2015) *Special Educational Needs and Disability: The Basics.* London: Routledge.

2 Working together: joint outcomes

This chapter provides:

- an understanding of relevant legislation including **must** and should statements within the 2015 SEND CoP;

- a consideration of the range of practitioners that the 2015 SEND CoP has relevance for;

- implications for joint working between all parties;

- an awareness of the rights of CnYP and their parents;

- an understanding of how different practitioners contribute to outcomes linked to the aspirations of CnYP.

Must and should statements

The 2015 SEND CoP provides guidance concerning legislation which **must** be considered by a wide range of practitioners and services. These **must** statements link to requirements of Part 3 of the Children and Families Act 2014.

Therefore, organisations are bound by legislation to 'have regard' to the 2015 SEND CoP when making decisions. 'They cannot ignore it' (DfE and DH, 2015, p 12). These organisations are required to demonstrate that the arrangements made for CnYP with SEN fulfil the statutory obligations the guidance seeks to outline.

Within the CoP are a number of statements where the word should is used. There is an expectation that such statements are adhered to. However, if there is any deviation from the CoP the organisation responsible is 'expected to explain any departure from it' (DfE and DH, 2015, p 12). Furthermore, to enable wider understanding and to support appropriate practice for CnYP with additional needs or disability, the CoP identifies additional legislation and guidance that may be helpful to all practitioners.

While the local authority (LA) **must** ensure that CnYP and their parents are fully included and consulted about the assessment process leading to an EHC plan, the CoP states that organisations should enable parents to share their unique knowledge of their CYPn and to know that their contributions are not only valued but acted upon. As a YPn reaches school leaving age, LAs and other organisations should normally transfer their engagement from the parent to the YPn themselves. Additionally, in order to further effective participation for the CYPn and their parent, LAs should work to build trust, making links with organisations and forums such as parent carer forums (PCFs).

Organisations that must have regard to the guidance in the SEND CoP

The scope of those for whom this document is relevant is wide, as can be seen in Figure 2.1. This diagram illustrates the plethora of organisations who '**must** *have regard to*' this statutory guidance (DfE and DH, 2015, p 13).

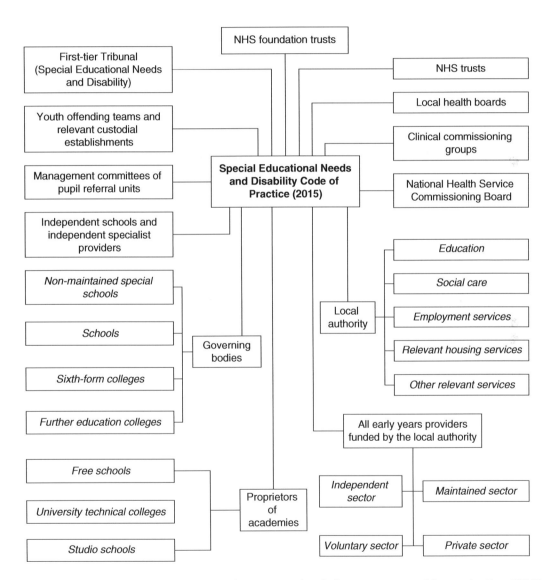

Figure 2.1 *Organisations who '***must*** have regard to' the statutory guidance in the SEND CoP 2015*

IMPLICATIONS FOR PRACTICE

Look at Figure 2.1 and consider the following questions.

*   Are there any organisations in this flow chart that you did not know were required to adhere to this guidance? Which are they and what difference will this knowledge make to your practice or expectations?

*   As a practitioner, who are the people you usually work with? Are there others who could enable your practice to be more effective?

*   Who are these people or organisations and what will you do to work collaboratively with them?

As can be seen by Figure 2.1, there is a wide range of different practitioners legally bound by the 2015 SEND CoP. Allan and Youdell (2017, p 76) identify the 'complex alliances' these present. These, along with individual priorities, budgetary constraints and the different ways of working of the practitioners involved, provide something of a challenge for joint working.

Working together in practice

The requirement for education, health and care to work together for joint outcomes is seen as fundamental to the 2015 SEND CoP. This CoP is a joint publication from the Department for Education (DfE) and the Department of Health (DH), therefore both education and health services are bound by the statutory requirements enshrined in this document. NHS England (2018a, p 7) reinforces the need for close working relationships between health, education and social care, advocating liaison between these services in order to ensure 'seamless support' for CnYP. Furthermore, Godson (2014) identifies the vital role of health workers such as paediatricians, therapists and specialist nurses such as health visitors and school nurses in maintaining effective professional contact with education and social care services.

Additionally, in guidance for FE and social care, the following identical paragraph occurs.

> Local Authorities must look to ensure integration between educational provision and training provision, health and social care provision where this would promote wellbeing and improve the quality of provision for disabled young people and those with SEN. This requires close co-operation with education, health and social care partners to research, plan and commission services.
>
> (DfE, 2014a, p 7; DfE, 2014b, p 8)

Such a clear obligation for strong joint working cannot be denied as the well being of CnYP is at stake.

Professional responsibilities for all parties

The Equality Act 2010 sets out a definition of disability as being a physical or mental impairment which has a long-term and adverse effect on the ability to carry out day-to-day activities. According to this legislation, all education providers and LAs **must not** directly or indirectly discriminate against any CYPn, but **must** make reasonable adjustments, including appropriate aids and services, in order for them not to be at a substantial disadvantage to their non-disabled peers. This includes an anticipatory duty, which involves the consideration of what might be required in advance, in order to prevent such disadvantage.

The public sector equality duty (Equality and Human Rights Commission, 2019) requires public bodies, as well as any other bodies with funding from the public purse such as independent specialist providers, to adhere to specific duties within the Equality Act 2010. They **must** publish their information showing compliance to this Act, with specific and measurable objectives. This is normally achieved via the Accessibility Plan which demonstrates how over time organisations plan strategically to increase accessibility. This is not limited to physical access but includes providing an accessible curriculum as well as information. Similarly, school governing bodies **must** publish their arrangements for the admission of disabled CnYP, including what will be provided to enable access to the curriculum, environment and information.

In specific terms, the LA **must** ensure that CnYP and their parents are fully included and consulted about the assessment process leading to an EHC plan and what that plan contains. This includes information on their rights and entitlements and should be timely and in accessible formats. As CnYP reach Year 9, education establishments and other agencies will begin planning for transition to adult life, including health, housing, finances, relationships and independence.

While Section 22 of the Children and Families Act 2014 makes it clear that LAs **must** operate in such a way as to identify all CnYP who have, or may have, SEN, Section 23 of the same Act outlines that clinical commissioning groups (CCG), National Health Service Trusts and NHS Foundation Trusts **must** inform the LA of any child they identify as having, or probably having, SEN as defined in the SEND CoP 2015. The Children and Families Act 2014 also supports the rights of the CYPn to mainstream education.

The rights of CnYP and their parents

As well as the actions that they **must** carry out, public bodies and individuals within them should be aware of and facilitate the rights of both CnYP and their parents. Articles 12 and 13 of the Convention on the Rights of the Child (United Nations, 1989) gives CnYP the right to give and receive information, to give an opinion and to have this considered, depending on their age, maturity and capability. In some cases, children may need support to be able to express their views, but the 2015 CoP states unequivocally that parents' views should not be used as an alternative to the voice of CnYP. The rights of the YP to express their own view must be upheld (DfE and DH, 2015, 1.10) and where there is any disagreement the YP's decision has legal precedence (DfE and DH, 2015, 2.13). The

CoP also states that YP **must** be confident that the advice and support they are receiving is treated confidentially, is impartial and should enable them to participate fully in the decision made. Where YP are undergoing transition assessments, the LA **must** provide independent advocacy (DfE and DH, 2015, 2.15).

While anyone can bring CnYP who they think may have SEN to the attention of the LA, it is the right of parents, YP themselves, schools and colleges to request an EHC assessment. Therefore, parents and their CYPn should feel able to tell their educational setting if they feel they may have SEN.

Working towards CnYP's aspirations

The 2015 SEND CoP outlines that CnYP, their parents and all other practitioners involved in working with the CnYP should have high aspirations leading towards successful outcomes in adult life. These ambitions relate to higher education and/or employment, independent living, participation in society and being a healthy adult (DfE and DH, 2015, 7.38). CnYP should be encouraged to make independent choices from an early age, including those relating to friendships, safety and health.

In the CoP, there is a shift away from narrow objectives and targets to an emphasis on outcomes. All practitioners working with CnYP with SEN are expected to know and understand the aspirations a CYPn may have for themselves and work towards this. However, an aspiration is not an outcome. The CoP defines an outcome as:

> the benefit or difference made to an individual as a result of an intervention. It should be personal and not expressed from a service perspective; it should be something that those involved have control and influence over, and while it does not always have to be formal or accredited, it should be specific, measurable, achievable, realistic and time bound (SMART).

> (DfE and DH, 2015, 9.66)

Therefore, outcomes should set out what needs to be achieved by the end of the key stage or phase of education and are steps towards a CYPn's own aspirations and what others judge to be important for them in the longer term.

For CnYP to achieve the best they can, all relevant services must work together to provide holistic support that enables CnYP to progress towards improved outcomes. While it is important for individual outcomes for CnYP to be identified and worked towards, it is also important for services to identify and work towards agreed outcomes and for attention also to be given to strategic level outcomes. Service level outcomes might include working towards improving the mental health of a designated number of CnYP, while strategic outcomes could be related to an increase in the percentage of young people (YP) supported into independent living. The joint commissioning of services for CnYP with SEN requires education, health and social care to work together in assessing the needs of CnYP and making decisions about how provision will be made for them. Each of these services has their own body to which they are accountable: examples include NHS England, Ofsted and the Director of Children's Services.

The Council for Disabled Children (CDC) has produced an excellent tool (see 'Critical Questions') to enable practitioners from education, health and social care, as well as parents, to identify outcomes for CnYP with SEN. This outcomes pyramid was devised following the findings from their 3-year Children's Outcomes Measurement Study (CHUMS) into health outcomes. Using this pyramid, CnYP can be supported to identify their long-term aspirations such as '*I want to be able to get a job*' or '*I want to go out on my own*'. Where the CYPn is not able to articulate aspirations for themselves, then aspirations should be identified using the best knowledge available of the CYPn.

From the identification of an aspiration, long-term outcomes such as '*improved confidence*', or '*improved social awareness and interaction*' are stated and agreed by all practitioners. Additionally, steps towards these outcomes are identified.

The needs of the CYPn are also identified across education, health and social care, such as '*difficulty with handling money*' or '*difficulty in managing anger*' and the provision to meet those needs should be clearly identified and articulated through the setting of clear targets. Such targets are short term and might include provision such as therapy from a member of the Child and Adolescent Mental Health Service (CAMHS), support from a teacher or teaching assistant (TA) in recognising money, or simple shopping activities.

SCENARIO

1. Chelsea is in Year 9. She attends school occasionally and finds having to make choices for her GCSEs overwhelming. She finds crowds difficult and does not make friends easily. She often stays in her room at home and self-harms. She spends a lot of time on the internet looking at fashion, hair styles and make up. Her aspiration is to become a fashion designer.

2. Alfie is 5 years old. He lives with foster parents. This is his third set of foster parents. He can have violent outbursts at school if other children don't play with him in the way he chooses; consequently, he does not have many friends. He has a short concentration span and is not working to expected levels in the classroom. Alfie's aspiration is to be a superhero with superpowers.

CRITICAL QUESTIONS

Use the CDC EHC outcomes pyramid at councilfordisabledchildren.org.uk/help-resources/resources/ehc-outcomes-pyramid to respond to the following questions.

- What outcome would you identify for Chelsea or Alfie (Section E of the pyramid)?
- What steps towards this outcome would you identify for health, education and social care?

→

- What would you consider Chelsea's or Alfie's EHC needs to be?
- What short-term targets would you set in each of these areas (Sections F, G and H of the pyramid) and who would be involved in carrying them out?

Conclusion

The 2015 CoP has required organisations across education, health and social care through legislation to collaborate more closely to ensure good outcomes for CnYP with SEN. There is a professional responsibility to make effective provision for such CnYP at both an individual and strategic level. We discuss SEN provision at a strategic level in Chapter 3.

Further reading and web-based materials

This article provides a critical examination of the CoP and aids the reader's understanding of the political context.

Burch, L F (2018) Governmentality of Adulthood: A Critical Discourse Analysis of the 2014 Special Educational Needs and Disability Code of Practice. *Disability and Society*, 33(1): 92–114.

This website is run by the umbrella body for the disabled children's sector, bringing together professionals, practitioners and policy-makers.

CDC: councilfordisabledchildren.org.uk/ (accessed 31 July 2019).

A website run by Nasen (National Association for Special Educational Needs). Plenty of material for a whole-school approach to supporting CnYP with SEN, with a very good section to support SENCOs.

SEND gateway: www.sendgateway.org.uk/ (accessed 26 November 2019).

3 Understanding the Local Offer

This chapter provides:

- an understanding of the purpose and remit of the Local Offer (LO);
- a discussion on commissioning across education, health and social care.

The purpose of the Local Offer

The Children and Families Act 2014 introduced a statutory duty for LAs stating they **must** develop, publish and review an LO that sets out the support expected to be available to those CnYP with SEND. It is important to note that this support is not just for CnYP who have EHC plans. The LO is something that parents and CnYP can refer to before, during and after identifying there is a SEN or disability. There is no need for a formal assessment to have taken place before the LO can be accessed. The LO has two key purposes.

1. *To provide clear, comprehensive, accessible and up-to-date information about the available provision and how to access it.*

2. *To make provision more responsive to local needs and aspirations by directly involving disabled children and those with SEN and their parents; and disabled young people (YP) and those with SEN, and service providers in its development and review.*

(DfE and DH, 2015, 4.2)

Legislation from the Equality Act 2010 also pertains to the LO, as do The Special Educational Needs and Disability Regulations (2014) Part 4.

Joint working, commissioning arrangements and understanding of outcomes across education, health and social care legislation span a period of 50 years. The table of legislation at the start of this book identifies the breadth of the legal framework that must be adhered to.

The 2015 CoP emphasises the importance of collaboration between education, health and social care services. This includes the joint commissioning of these services. There is a need for high quality commissioning arrangements within and beyond each local area. These arrangements are best achieved through a co-ordinated joint commissioning cycle with a direct line of sight from an individual CYPn through to area-wide commissioning. To enable CnYP, families and agencies to navigate their way through commissioned provision, the LO should provide all necessary information in one place.

The remit of the Local Offer

The SEND CoP 4.7 states that the LO should adhere to the following principles.

It should be:

- collaborative and **must** involve parents and CnYP in both the preparation and review;

- accessible, easy to understand, factual and jargon free;

- comprehensive and **must** include eligibility criteria for services where relevant;

- up to date;

- transparent.

Figure 3.1 illustrates the information that must be provided on each LA's LO. The Special Educational Needs and Disability Regulations (2014) provide a common framework for this.

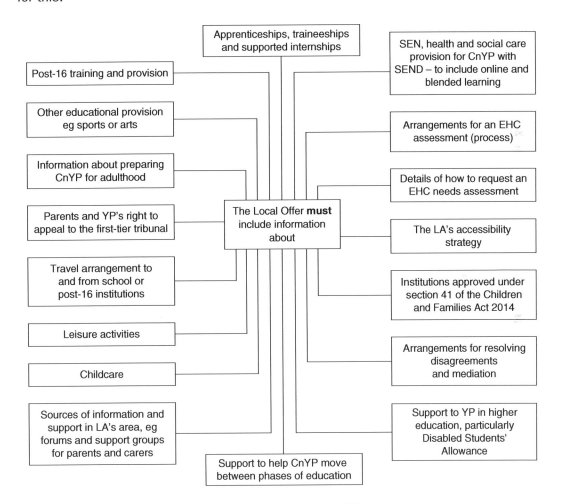

Figure 3.1 *Information that **must** be included in a Local Offer*

The Local Offer and commissioning services

The 2015 CoP places much greater emphasis on procurement and commissioning of service; both terms were seldom mentioned in previous versions. Local partners, such as the LA and health authority, are tasked with commissioning services to meet the CnYP's SEN and disabilities. CnYP, their families and PCFs hold a key role in informing these arrangements at all levels. Family experience, ambitions and expectations should be shared on both an individual and strategic level. This shared activity should change the power relationships between the parties. It seeks to ensure that CnYP and parents, who are experts by experience, have an equal role. All parties contribute to the process of understanding local needs, as well as developing innovative solutions to address them. The language used in the CoP, however, is quite businesslike, using terminology such as providers, services, joint arrangements and joint outcomes. Such language may not be accessible to all.

Commissioning can be defined as '*to order or authorise the production of (something)*' (Lexico, 2019). Its Latin origins refer to '*the delegation of business*' (Etymonline, 2019). SEN commissioning requires health, education, social care, private and voluntary sectors to co-ordinate their arrangements. This involves diverse procurement and contractual arrangements. While the CoP requires SEN commissioning to secure effective provision, it does not articulate the monetary cost (Allan and Youdell, 2017).

The CoP would appear to hide in plain sight the *business* of commissioning. The diversity and choice available within the education sector creates a model of private sector competition and entrepreneurship in a context of austerity (Lehane, 2017). Commissioners have to ask uncomfortable questions about what can be afforded. The meeting of CnYP's assessed needs effectively should not be driven by the availability of services, nor should the associated costs fall to one agency. A question is raised as to whether this may compromise the provision required to meet the whole spectrum of the CYPn's needs.

Commissioning decisions should be informed by a clear assessment of local needs including the Joint Strategic Needs Assessment (JSNA) (LA, social care and health) and the Joint Health and Wellbeing Board (NHS, social care and public health). Such decisions are designed to achieve the best use of all resources available to improve outcomes efficiently, equitably, effectively and sustainably (SEND CoP, 3.7). Joint commissioning should secure personalised and integrated provision and consider transition points between educational settings, particularly in preparing for adulthood. Provision commissioned by other agencies, such as schools and other educational settings, should also be taken into account. This complex shared remit must seek to avoid duplication and gaps.

The SEND CoP (3.18) states that parents and CnYP with SEN **must** be involved in sharing their experiences, ambitions and expectations, in order to improve commissioning decisions. The Brighton and Hove SEND inspection outcome letter (Ofsted, 2018) identified effective joint commissioning, where the strong vision of the local area leaders was described as family centred with effective working relationships. Key elements identified were shared trust, openness and transparency. Where joint commissioning is less effective, through a lack of co-ordinated understanding of CnYP's EHC needs, then CnYP are being left without the services they require.

The Local Offer website

The LO is designed to provide easy access to comprehensive information and make provision more responsive to local needs and aspirations. Websites have been developed collaboratively in each local area to address this duty. However, Allan and Youdell (2017) identified that there is an overreliance on signposting and that fragmentation of information has made navigating the system difficult. They go on to identify that '*the local state is at once responsibilised and stripped of both autonomy to design or deliver and of the resources to fund while open to challenge by non-state entities*' (p 77).

The recent Education Committee report into SEND (House of Commons, 2019a, p 4) recommends that LOs should be reviewed in collaboration with CnYP and their parents as their findings identify that LOs have not delivered as intended and that in some cases they were '*unsuitable and useless*'.

SCENARIO

Connor's EHC plan identifies the need for a very high level of support from education, health and social care in order to secure Preparing for Adulthood outcomes. Connor is 21. His mother is in the Royal Air Force. She is requesting an out-of-authority specialist residential placement.

CRITICAL QUESTIONS

Using the internet, find the LO for the area where you live. Use this information to respond to the following questions.

- What will have informed mum's choice of placement and how will she know it will meet Connor's needs?

- What information is available from the LO about EHC provision to support preparation for adulthood?

IMPLICATIONS FOR PRACTICE

- From the perspective of your own practice, in what ways does the LO influence your work with CnYP and their families?

- As a practitioner, do you see commissioning in your local area reflecting family experience, ambitions and expectations, at both individual and strategic levels?

Conclusion

The LO is a statutory requirement introduced through the 2015 SEND CoP with the intention of it providing a one-stop shop of all services available to support CnYP and their families. It is intended to enable innovative and collaborative working practice with families to shape the joint commissioning of provision at an individual and strategic level. The challenge remains in ensuring it is fully accessible and fully reflective of local need.

Further reading and web-based materials

A report for parents whose children have additional needs, indicating that information provided in LOs is worryingly patchy and varies significantly across LAs. It makes a number of helpful recommendations regarding childcare for CnYP with SEN.

Family and Childcare Trust (2017) *Childcare for All: The Role of the Local Offer.* [online] Available at: www.familyandchildcaretrust.org/childcare-all-role-local-offer (accessed 13 August 2019).

This fact sheet provides you with details of what is meant by commissioning and who would be involved, including a range of services.

Working Together: Joint Commissioning Arrangements. [online] Available at: council fordisabledchildren.org.uk/sites/default/files/field/attachemnt/MIH_Working%20 togehter.pdf (assessed 10 August 2019).

PART TWO KNOWING THE CHILD OR YOUNG PERSON

4 Early identification: universal provision

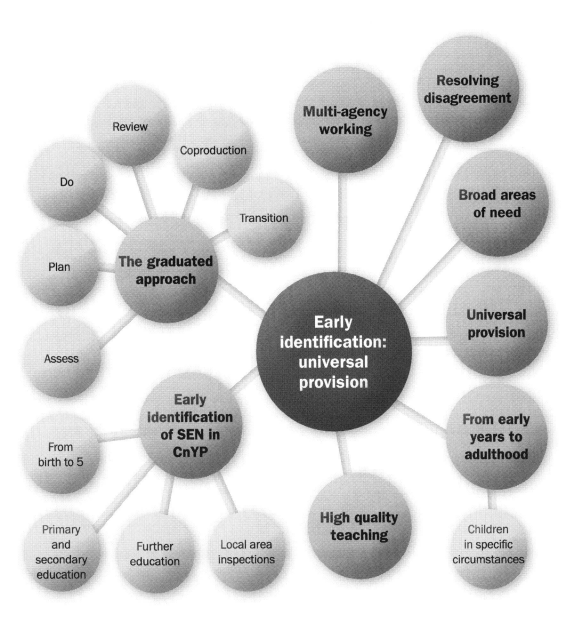

This chapter provides:

- an understanding of assessing and identifying individual need throughout a child or YPn's educational journey;

- an understanding of the roles and responsibilities of LAs in identifying and supporting CnYP with SEN;

- an exploration of high quality teaching, including the assess, plan, do, review approach or graduated response;

- a consideration of specific groups of CnYP;

- an outline of the first steps towards resolving disagreement.

Universal provision

While the term universal provision is commonly used, interestingly the CoP does not use this, preferring instead to use the term high quality teaching. Universal provision is that which is commonly available to all CnYP. This means being able to make use of a range of services from education, health and/or social care that are available to all CnYP and their families. These services can be accessed without needing any specialist resources or assessment and the LO should identify the universal provision that is made available.

From early years to adulthood

Chapters 5, 6 and 7 of the revised SEND CoP 2015 provide an overview of processes concerning the identification of SEN and the provision that should be made for CnYP. These chapters provide information for all education providers from early years to a wide range of post-16 provision including both the private and voluntary sector.

Understanding and assessing any CYPn's individual needs from an education, health or care perspective can occur at any point in their lives. For some CnYP evidence of SEN is clear from an early age, while for others this may not become apparent until later.

Health services support early identification of young children who may have SEN, through neonatal screening programmes, the Healthy Child Programme and specialist health and developmental assessments where concerns may be raised. Practitioners in these services are often the first people to notify LAs about young children with SEN.

For CnYP who are looked after or who have child protection or children in need status, considerable planning is required to ensure care, health and educational needs are met. For all CnYP who have social care plans, careful consideration should be given to integrating assessment processes across all disciplines.

Identifying need at the earliest point, and then making effective provision, improves long-term outcomes for CnYP. Parents know their CYPn best and it is important that all practitioners listen and understand when parents express concerns about their child's development. They should also ensure they actively listen to and address any concerns raised by CnYP themselves. As previously stated in Chapter 1, the Lamb Report (Department for Children, Schools and Families, 2009) recognised that parents need to be listened to in order to facilitate partnership with statutory bodies in a more meaningful way.

The expectations of the Equality Duty (Equality and Human Rights Commission, 2019) indicate that throughout every CYPn's journey, from early years to post-16 education, they must be given equality of opportunity consistent with inclusive practice. All schools and educational settings **must** make reasonable adjustments for CnYP to prevent them from '*being put at a substantial disadvantage*' (SEND CoP, 5.10, 6.9 and 7.7). These duties are anticipatory. Schools **must** provide information about their arrangements for making provision for CnYP with SEN. This includes admission and accessibility arrangements as well as what is in place to prevent CnYP with SEN being treated less favourably than other pupils (SEND CoP, 4.35).

Additionally, schools and educational settings **must** co-operate with the LA in the consideration of provision of support through the LO. The Equality Act 2010 also outlines a legal obligation for all public authorities, including health and social care, to provide services to meet the diverse needs of their users. In education this is achieved via an annually published accessibility strategy. As we detail in Chapter 2, this requires all public bodies, such as schools, colleges, local education authorities (LEA) and all other education providers, to publish plans for physical access and access to the curriculum.

CRITICAL QUESTIONS

Find the website that publishes your LA's LO and locate the accessibility strategy.

*   What information does the strategy provide?

*   How would you expect education providers to implement the strategy?

*   What additional services might be required to enable the accessibility strategy to be effective?

It is important to recognise that there are groups of CnYP with complex needs who will benefit from any of the education, health and social care services. Where CnYP have medical conditions, the Children and Families Act 2014 requires schools and education settings to support such CnYP through an individual health care plan (HCP) which specifies the type and level of health support needed. This is underpinned through the statutory guidance *Supporting Pupils at School with Medical Conditions* (DfE, 2015). Where such CnYP are also considered to have SEN or a disability, it is vital for their provision to be planned and delivered in a way that takes account of both their health needs and their SEN. This would also apply to social care needs where appropriate. Parents should be informed when special educational provision is being made for their CYPn (SEND CoP, 6.43).

Children in specific circumstances

Another group of CnYP identified within Chapter 10 of the CoP are those in specific circumstances. These include, for example, looked-after children, CnYP in youth custody and children of service personnel. We examine their needs in more detail in later chapters. However, it is important to recognise other diverse groups who are not specifically mentioned in the CoP. These include refugees, travellers, CnYP who are trafficked or LGBT+, and young carers, who may or may not have additional SEN. The circumstances of these groups of CnYP may present challenges for both the CnYP and those who know them, and which may or may not affect their learning and socialisation. The educational setting these CnYP attend should be aware of such implications and provide for them within universal support and by making use of what is made available across education, health and social care through the LO.

High quality teaching

High quality teaching is teaching which should be universally available to all CnYP. It is what is provided every day to every CYPn by their teachers and should ensure that high expectations are set for every pupil whatever their prior attainment. Teachers should use appropriate assessment to set targets that are deliberately ambitious. Potential areas of difficulty should be identified and addressed at the outset. Lessons should be planned to address potential areas of difficulty and to remove barriers to CnYP's achievement. High quality teaching is recognised as being both cost-effective and sustainable in terms of addressing the broad range of additional needs (DfE, 2017a, p 46).

High quality teaching at its most effective ensures good differentiation: closely matching teaching to individual CnYP in order to personalise teaching and learning approaches. The SEND CoP states, '*additional intervention and support cannot compensate for a lack of good quality teaching*' (6.37). If you are a CYPn receiving high quality teaching, you should expect to experience approaches that include:

- individual or group support as appropriate;
- visual supports;
- tasks carefully matched to need;
- success built into tasks to give confidence and reduce any risk of failure;
- introduction of new skills in small steps, starting from what is already known;
- practical demonstration;
- the generalisation of skill to other tasks where appropriate;
- ensuring attention has been gained before trying to teach a new skill;
- keeping careful records to ensure continuity and progression;
- realistic time targets for completing work;
- frequent use of praise and relevant rewards;

- immediate feedback, positively framed;

- evaluation and review of work set and the achievement made;

- accommodation of different learning styles.

(Adapted from DfE, 2017a, p 14)

IMPLICATIONS FOR PRACTICE

Consider a CYPn you work with in your role as an education practitioner such as teacher, lecturer, key worker or TA.

- Using your knowledge of this individual, which of the approaches above have you found effective in enabling the CYPn to achieve their best?

- What other approaches might you offer in order for the CYPn to fulfil their potential?

- How will you support all CnYP you work with to '*become confident individuals living fulfilling lives*' (SEND CoP, 6.1)?

Early identification of SEN in CnYP

One of the key principles of the 2015 CoP is

> *the early identification of children and young people's needs and early interven-
> tion to support them*

(DfE and DH, 2015, 1.2)

The early identification of a CYPn's SEN is an important first step in providing relevant support to enable progress academically, socially and emotionally, and to enable the realisation of aspirations. However, there is a possible contradiction to be aware of. Early provision and support may depend on early identification and might include diagnosis. This could be the first opportunity for a label to be given to CnYP, especially in the early years. It is often a health practitioner (HP) such as a health visitor carrying out health screening and developmental checks who may identify a need. However, the absence of a label or diagnosis should not prevent early provision being put in place once a need has been identified. As Section 23 of the Children and Families Act 2014 states, if a child under school age is considered by the HP to have SEN, it is the responsibility of the health authority to talk with parents about their concerns and to provide support. Parents should be signposted to other sources of aid prior to the child entering early years provision or beginning school.

CRITICAL QUESTIONS

You are a parent and you have concerns about your 2-year-old's communication and inter-action with their peers. Consider the following questions.

*   Who do you share your concerns with?

*   What are the mechanisms for doing this?

*   How much information do you think is relevant to share?

*   What are the implications, both positive and negative, of sharing this information?

From birth to 5

Complex developmental and sensory needs may be identified during pregnancy or at birth. Advances in science and technology are enabling a wider range of tests to be made *in utero*. However, parents' early observations of their child are also crucial and the SEND CoP (5.14) consistently recognises the part they play in the contribution of information and opinion.

The Early Years Foundation Stage (EYFS) statutory framework (DfE, 2017c) sets out a clear requirement to have measures in place to assess SEN as part of the setting's overall approach to monitoring the progress and development of all children. The progress check carried out between the ages of 2 and 3 is the first formal assessment point after birth when the child's progress and development is formally reported on to parents. It focuses on communication and language, physical development and personal, social and emotional development. It should highlight areas where:

*   good progress is being made;

*   some additional support might be needed;

*   there is a concern that a child may have a developmental delay (which may indicate SEN or disability).

Primary and secondary education

In primary and secondary settings, the progress of all CnYP is assessed and monitored. If progress is less than expected, the CoP (6.17) identifies four key factors that help determine whether SEN provision is required. These are demonstrated by progress that:

*   is significantly slower than their peers;

*   fails to match the child's previous rate of progress;

*   does not close the attainment gap between them and their peers;

*   widens the attainment gap.

As in the early years, a CYPn's progress is not just considered in academic terms, but also in terms of wider development or social needs (SEND CoP, 6.18).

Further education

YP entering FE may already have had their SEN identified. However, for some YP their SEN may emerge in the FE or college setting. The SEND CoP (7.3) clearly identifies that such FE providers, including colleges, sixth-form colleges and 16–19 academies, have a duty to use their best endeavours to secure the special educational provision that meets the YPn's needs. Colleges should give all applicants opportunity, before or at entry and at subsequent points, to declare whether they have a learning need, a disability or a medical condition that will affect their learning.

It is important to recognise that early identification can happen at any point of a CYPn's educational journey. You can see how this might be played out through the following scenarios.

SCENARIO

Choose one of the following:

1. Jayden is in his first year in post-16 education. His aspiration is to be a motor mechanic. He has been diagnosed as having dyslexia and attention deficit hyperactivity disorder (ADHD). He finds concentration difficult and does not always take his medication. He does not always make good friendship choices and is often tired. His grandmother takes him to college every day by car, but both the college and his house are on a bus route.

2. Chelsea is in Year 9. She attends school occasionally and finds having to make choices for her GCSEs overwhelming. She finds crowds difficult and does not make friends easily. She often stays in her room at home and self-harms. She spends a lot of time on the internet looking at fashion, hair styles and make up. Her aspiration is to become a fashion designer.

IMPLICATIONS FOR PRACTICE

Thinking about early identification, answer the following questions.

* Whose voice do you think is important in determining aspiration and why?

* What practitioner partnerships would be appropriate to form? Why?

* Who would you ask to gather initial information about the CYPn's strengths and areas of need?

Local area inspections

Since 2016, the joint DfE and Care Quality Commission (CQC) local area inspections of SEN have reported on three key aspects in each local area; the first being the effectiveness of the local area in identifying CnYP who have SEN and/or disabilities. The inspection pays particular attention to how well:

- local agencies and bodies plan and co-ordinate their work to assess need;
- local agencies and bodies provide necessary and effective support;
- the local area involves the individual CYPn and their parents in the process of assessing their needs.

The outcome letter published following each joint local area inspection, identifying strengths and required actions about early identification of need, is made available on LO websites and is therefore a public document.

CRITICAL QUESTIONS

Find the outcome letter following the joint DfE and CQC inspection for your local area by searching your LO website. Consider the following questions.

- What are the strengths and areas for development concerning early identification of SEN from this inspection?

- What are the implications of the inspection findings for a CYPn you are familiar with?

The graduated approach

Most CnYP's SEN can be met within universal, targeted and bespoke provision. DfE data (DfE, 2019a) shows that 85 per cent of all CnYP are not considered to have SEN whereas 11.9 per cent are receiving SEN support. This includes both targeted and bespoke provision. Only 3.1 per cent of CnYP with SEN have an EHC plan.

When a CYPn is identified as having SEN, educational settings should seek to remove barriers to learning via the graduated approach. This ensures that the CYPn's needs become more fully understood, and identifies what supports good progress and how good outcomes maybe secured.

As more and more information is gathered, different approaches may be implemented and more specialist input offered. Conversely, if the provision that has been put in place is effective in enabling progress, then it may be maintained, reduced or ceased.

The CoP makes it clear that 'high quality teaching differentiated for individual pupils is the first step in responding to pupils who have or may have SEN' (DfE and DH, 2015, 6.37). In order to ensure that CnYP can make good progress and secure outcomes, a four-part cycle known as the graduated approach should be implemented; this involves the assess, plan, do, review cycle.

Assess

The purpose of assessment by education settings is to identify need, provide appropriate support and monitor the progress of CnYP across a range of broad areas of development. Assessment is carried out to see what CnYP know, understand and can do. As part of the information gathering at this stage, the views and experiences of the parent as well as the CnYP should be considered (SEND CoP, 6.45). These views, together with information from screening or assessment, contribute to a holistic understanding of need and therefore inform the planning of appropriate provision. If health and social services are already involved with a CYPn, they should also liaise with school and contribute to the assessment of the CYPn's progress and development.

IMPLICATIONS FOR PRACTICE

Consider the following.

As a practitioner from health, education or social care:

*   what information would you need to determine whether a CYPn has made appropriate progress?

*   who else would you consult with to inform the assessment process?

For CnYP who have English as an additional language (EAL), careful consideration needs to be made as to whether presenting difficulties are as a result of language limitations or SEN. The CoP (6.24) categorically states '*difficulties related solely to limitations in English as an additional language are not SEN*'.

Plan

Once the information gathered from assessments indicates that additional support is needed, the teacher, the CYPn and parents should agree on desired outcomes along with the strategies and approaches to be used to meet those outcomes. The SENCO from the educational setting may also be involved. All parties should be completely aware of the nature of the support being planned and parents should, where possible, reinforce these approaches at home (CoP, 6.51).

Do

The vast majority of CnYP should be able to have their needs met through high quality teaching. The class or subject teacher should remain responsible for working with the CYPn on a daily basis. Any additional adults within the classroom should be deployed in

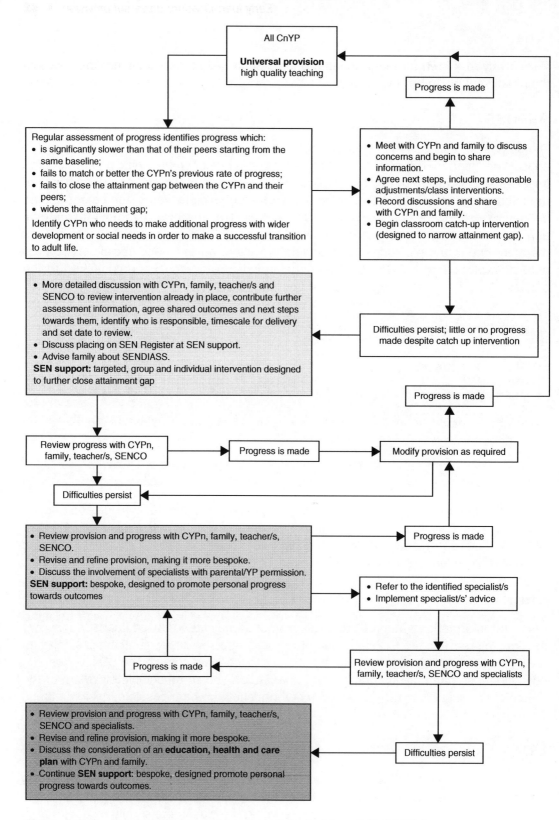

Figure 4.1 *The graduated approach process (adapted from DfE, 2017a)*

such a way that the individual needs are met. Such needs also include wider developmental, health and care requirements. The teacher should ensure that what has been agreed in the planning meeting with parents and the CYPn is implemented and that any progress towards agreed outcomes is documented (CoP, 6.52).

Review

It is important that the support offered through high quality teaching is reviewed and the CYPn's progress towards the agreed outcomes is monitored. The effectiveness of the strategies and approaches employed should be analysed and changes and adaptations agreed by all parties involved. If it is considered that the support that has been put in place through universal provision has enabled the CYPn to make progress, then this provision will be maintained or modified. The cycle of assess, plan, do, review will be repeated. If after review it is considered that the support that has been put in place has not been sufficient to enable progress then it may be decided to offer additional, targeted intervention. Since such provision is '*different from or additional to*' that available to the CYPn's peers (CoP, 6.15), this formally identifies the CYPn as having SEN. As can be seen from this discussion, determining whether a CYPn is considered to have SEN is a complex matter.

Once the assess, plan, do and review cycle has identified that less than expected progress has been made, a process of revisiting, refining and revising earlier decisions should result in effective special educational provision. This is illustrated in Figure 4.1.

As Figure 4.1 shows, the assess, plan, do, review cycle is integral in making effective provision for CnYP beyond the identification of SEN. We discuss this more fully in Chapters 5 and 6.

Coproduction

The involvement of CnYP and their parents is a strong principle of the SEND CoP 2015. Coproduction is an approach which views all those involved in the provision for a CYPn as equal, regardless of professional status. It sees those who use health, education or social care services as having knowledge and lived experience which can be used to improve service delivery. It involves the sharing of power in assessing, planning and carrying out provision and support. Coproduction can be implemented at many levels such as the co-construction of policy and strategy through the LO, as well as with individual CnYP and their families. It is used across a range of public and voluntary sectors, including health, education and social care.

A report into the practice of coproduction across public services identified six elements as vital to the process of coproduction. These were:

- *building on people's capabilities;*
- *mutuality and reciprocity;*
- *encouraging the building of peer support networks;*
- *blurring boundaries between delivering and receiving services;*
- *facilitating rather than delivering;*
- *recognising people as assets.*

(Boyle et al, 2010)

Effective coproduction therefore relies on the recognition that all those involved in the partnership have ability and can be supported to fulfil this. It requires the sharing of benefits and skills and the valuing of peer networks alongside support from professionals. The distinction between those giving the service and those receiving the service should be blurred with more emphasis on how things can be achieved. Services should encourage the empowerment of others to make things happen rather than doing things to or for those accessing their services. In this way people are seen as active partners and not beneficiaries or burdens to the system.

Coproduction as an approach is highlighted in the annual report of the National Network of Parent Carer Forums (NNPCF) (Contact, 2017), which considers parent/carer participation across England. In a monitoring activity, PCFs were asked to comment on the extent to which they thought they coproduce with colleagues in health, education and social care. In data, which has been collected since 2011–12, a spike in rates at which they coproduced with education partners was reached in 2013–14, and while the rate of coproduction in education seems to have dropped, it was still higher than for health or social care in 2015–16. Coproduction rates with health began at a lower point in 2011–12 but the latest available figures showed an upward trend, whereas coproduction rates with social care show little change over time. Thus, while the CoP advocates the principles of coproduction, the practice of coproduction is yet to be fully embedded in practice across all services. Working with parents and their CnYP as full partners is crucial to effective provision for CnYP's needs. It builds trust and respect between all parties and has the potential to bring about significant benefits both in the present and for the future.

Transition

Transition in an educational context is commonly understood as the process whereby a CYPn moves between educational phases. It is important to also recognise that for any CYPn transition or change may occur on a daily basis, for example from classroom to classroom, from adult to adult, from indoors to outdoors, or structured to unstructured times. Some CnYP may find such changes difficult and may require support. At any stage where a CYPn moves from one phase of education to another, or from one kind of provision to another, there should be a carefully planned transition process so that all relevant information is passed on and appropriate further assessment of need can be gained.

However, the removal of national assessment levels for primary-aged children in 2015 gave schools the freedom to create their own systems to record progress. This can mean that information sharing between settings can be problematic since there is no universally consistent method of recording progress. Equally of fundamental importance is the principle that CnYP and their parents should be involved in the coproduction of a transition plan thus helping to aid a smooth transition between settings.

Multi-agency working

While the CoP provides the current framework for early identification, support and working together, this is not a new approach. The CDC ran an Early Support programme (2002–15) aimed at improving the way in which services worked with disabled CnYP and their families. A key aim was to bring together practitioners from education, health and social care to work collaboratively in the best interests of the CYPn. This programme of early support was underpinned by the following ten principles:

1. valued uniqueness;
2. planning partnerships;
3. key working;
4. birth to adulthood;
5. learning and development;
6. informed choices;
7. ordinary lives;
8. participation;
9. working together;
10. workforce development.

While these recommendations were specifically written with disabled children in mind, some of whom may have been identified before entering school or have an already identified SEN, they seem to capture the essence of early identification and support in order to help achieve aspirations.

IMPLICATIONS FOR PRACTICE

Look at the list above and think about the questions from your own position as a practitioner.

- Which of these recommendations for working collaboratively are prioritised within your area of practice and why?

- Which recommendations would benefit from further development and how could you further this development?

Resolving disagreement

If views and opinions differ and parents feel the needs of their CYPn are not being considered or addressed, the first steps to resolving disagreement might include conversations with the class or subject teacher or another universal provider, for example a health visitor or school nurse. It is important for all practitioners to have open and honest conversations, using active listening to overcome any real or perceived barriers. Successful early discussions will ensure that disagreements can be readily resolved.

Broad areas of need

Having identified that a CYPn is considered to have SEN, it is important to match the provision offered to the need identified. Chapter 6 (6.28–6.35) of the CoP provides details of the main categories of need for CnYP in schools. However, there is no explicit reference to categories of need within the chapter on FE in the CoP (Chapter 7).

The four categories are:

- communication and interaction, which includes speech, language and communication needs, Asperger's syndrome and autism;

- cognition and learning, which includes children who learn more slowly than others, those with moderate learning difficulties, severe learning difficulties (SLD) and profound and multiple learning difficulties (PMLD) as well as those with specific learning difficulties (SpLD) such as dyslexia and dyspraxia;

- social, emotional and mental health difficulties, which includes anxiety, depression, ADHD and attachment disorder;

- sensory and/or physical needs, which includes visual impairment, hearing impairment and multisensory impairment.

Some CnYP may have needs in more than one area and the schools' DfE termly census requires categorisation of SEN needs in up to two main areas of need, ranked in order of significance. For settings and schools, the purpose of these four broad categories of need is much less to label the child as to make suitable provision for them. Such provision should enable positive outcomes to be achieved and ensure that the gap between an individual and their peers does not widen as a result of late identification of need. This is essential if the traditional 'wait-to-fail' model of provision is to be avoided (Frederickson and Cline, 2015, p 136).

Conclusion

Universal provision requires all CnYP regardless of their age and educational setting to be placed at the centre of any information gathering and decision-making. A robust approach to this should ensure individual needs are recognised early so that appropriate provision can be put in place. However, the complexities of communication and collaboration between all practitioners may become apparent. This is examined further in subsequent chapters.

Further reading and web-based materials

This is a reader-friendly booklet particularly for education staff. It provides practical guidance on how to implement the graduated approach and how to engage parents effectively.

Nasen (2014) *SEN Support and the Graduated Approach. A Quick Guide to Ensuring That Every Child or Young Person Gets the Support they Require to Meet their Needs.* Tamworth: Nasen.

This provides the reader with research-based evidence for what makes great teaching and how to promote better learning. It also describes tools to help achieve this.

Sutton Trust (2014) *What Makes Great Teaching?* [online] Available at: www.suttontrust. com/wp-content/uploads/2014/10/What-makes-great-teaching-FINAL-4.11.14-1.pdf (accessed 16 September 2019).

This YouTube clip is an excellent 15-minute explanation of how coproduction has been enacted between those offering services and those accessing such services.

Contact a Family: www.youtube.com/watch?v=SPa3qrDZWp8 (accessed 17 June 2019).

5 Providing support: targeted provision

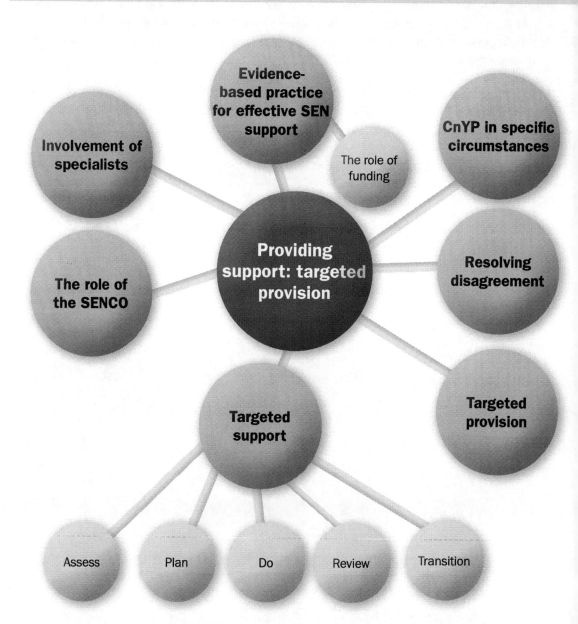

This chapter provides:

- an understanding of targeted support beyond universal provision;

- consideration of the role of the SENCO;

- information about evidence-based practice for effective support;

- a consideration of the role of funding.

Targeted provision

As we discussed in Chapter 4, many CnYP's learning needs can and should be met through access to high quality teaching and universally available services. However, once SEN have been identified, SEN support should be initiated. The assess, plan, do, review cycle becomes the primary process for ensuring that the CYPn is enabled to achieve identified outcomes and that any barriers to learning are removed. Shared discussions with all practitioners, with the voice of the CYPn and their family being at the heart of these discussions, should inform robust practice.

SEN support is intended to operate as a dynamic model and Figure 5.1 demonstrates the potential movement between different layers of support, both for an increased level of support, and for reducing support should this no longer be required. It is not a one-way pathway but rather seeks to respond flexibly to individual CnYP's needs, which are likely to vary over time, age and stage of education.

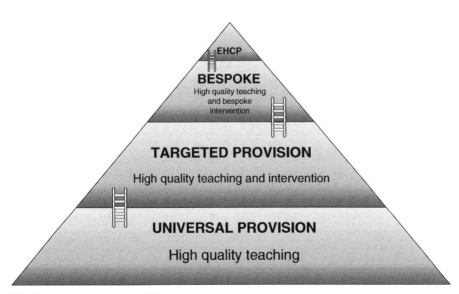

Figure 5.1 *Targeted provision: SEN support*

Targeted support

It is important to seek the CYPn's views when providing targeted support. This is known as person-centred planning (PCP). The principle of PCP is made clear in the Children and Families Act 2014. This approach is recognised as a collection of tools based upon a set of shared values that can be used to plan *with* a person – not *for* them. The DH (2010, p 12) defines PCP as '*a way of asking what people want, the support they need and how they can get it*'. It is about recognising what that CYPn brings, their strengths, what we can work with and what their contribution to society might be. The SEND CoP states, '*The support provided to an individual should always be based on a full understanding of their particular strengths and needs and seek to address them all using well evidenced interventions targeted at their areas of difficulty and where necessary specialist equipment or software*' (DfE and DH, 2015, 6.27).

This person-centred approach requires educators and services to move beyond a deficit focus whereby the expectation is that the CYPn must fit into existing approaches or accept the limitations that exist. This model of disability often comprises tests designed to reach a failure point and the associated impersonal language – such as referral, diagnosis, treatment, casework, client, service user – often used by services. While not explicitly stated within the CoP, there is an implicit understanding of the values of a person-centred approach and that services should work together with this in mind. We discuss this further in Chapter 6.

IMPLICATIONS FOR PRACTICE

Watch the first 5 minutes 41 seconds of the following clip from Inclusive Solutions, which explains what PCP is: https://inclusive-solutions.com/person-centred-planning.

From your own practitioner perspective, consider the following.

* Reflect on your understanding of PCP. How does this differ to those discussed on the video clip? Why might that be?

* What would you need to do to create a space where everyone feels safe and able to participate?

* How would you support the CYPn to be at the centre of the process?

Assess

At SEN support, as in universal provision, further assessment can take many forms and be both formal and informal in nature. This information gathering typically might consist of analysis of progress data, observation of the CYPn in the learning environment and discussions, including with the parents and CYPn. Other pertinent information, eg SEN checklists, audits of need, formal screening tools, standardised tests and diagnostic assessments may also be considered. At this early stage of identification of SEN, contributions towards the assessment process are likely to be made by universal providers across education, health and social care. The intention is to secure a holistic understanding of the individual CYPn. Factors such as health needs, attendance or behaviour should also be considered as they might indicate barriers to learning.

The Children Act 1989 recognises children with disabilities as *'children in need'*. Social care support should be given to the child and family as soon as a need is identified and should not wait until the completion of an EHC plan needs assessment. Evidence from national data (DfE, 2018a; DfE, 2019b) indicates that CnYP educated at SEN support are more likely to have their needs overlooked, be excluded and achieve less well than those who hold an EHC plan.

The CoP (7.10) states that at any point during FE a YPn should have the opportunity to declare they may have a learning need, disability or health condition that may affect their learning. This may or may not equate with a professional diagnosis. Documentation should be kept of this information and an assessment may be undertaken to inform provision required. The use of a person-centred approach at this early stage should ensure that the CYPn and their parents are empowered to contribute to a partnership that seeks to achieve positive change through removal of barriers.

SCENARIO

David is 7 years old and attends his local primary school. In some areas of the curriculum he is not meeting age-related expectations. His parents do not engage with the school.

When collecting information to seek to understand David's needs, it has been difficult to gain the family perspective and involvement.

IMPLICATIONS FOR PRACTICE

From the perspective of your own practice, consider the following.

* What skills might you need to effectively engage David's parents to support his progress and development?

* What barriers, such as parental lack of engagement, may need to be addressed in planning future provision?

* What assessments, formal and informal, could you carry out within your area of practice to inform decisions about support to enable David to make progress in his learning?

CnYP's needs may not be immediately obvious or may occur in more than one area of SEN. All practitioners should remain open-minded about any categorisation of SEN and ensure that the CnYP's needs are considered holistically. A CYPn, for example, who exhibits significant social, emotional and mental health needs may be masking an unmet need such as dyslexia; or a CYPn displaying autism type behaviours may have a cerebral visual impairment that outwardly manifests itself with similar symptoms to autism. Co-occurrence (the existence of two or more conditions at the same time) is also recognised; for example, the links between autism and ADHD or autism and epilepsy. However, the annual School Census data collection point that informs both the DfE and Department of Health and Social Care (DHSC) rely upon the CYPn's primary SEN being identified and is reliant upon education settings making an accurate assessment of primary need.

Plan

Once the assessment phase evidences the need to provide SEN support, the parents should be notified formally that SEN provision is being made (CoP, 6.2). CnYP and parents should be made aware of the LA's independent Information, Advice and Support Service, often known as SENDIASS, as detailed in LO websites. As at universal provision, the planning phase is informed by the information gathered through the assessment process. This could include, for example, reports from a teacher of the deaf, a speech and language therapist (SALT), a school nurse or an Early Help family support worker. Implementing the report recommendations and taking into account the CYPn and family voice, specific outcomes are identified and agreed. Such outcomes can be defined as the benefit or difference made to an individual as a result of the agreed actions and include attention to holistic progress, development and/or behaviour. The agreed actions will include adjustments, interventions and support and contribute to the achievement of the outcomes.

Do

Targeted support for the CYPn may be delivered in a group, one to one, online or with teachers, TAs or specialist staff such as a specialist teacher for visually or hearing-impaired pupils, SALT, occupational therapist (OT) or physiotherapist. It is important to recognise that the class or subject teacher remains responsible for the progress and wider development of the CYPn. Interventions delivered should have a reliable evidence of effectiveness (Mitchell, 2013) and be provided by staff possessing sufficient skills and knowledge.

There are many nationally recognised organisations that offer further advice and support for settings, CnYP and families around specific areas of SEN. Many of those, together with regional and local organisations, should be located on each area's LO website.

CRITICAL QUESTIONS

The following four organisations are listed in the web-based materials at the end of this chapter and can be found in Annex Two of the CoP.

- The Autism Education Trust (AET)

- The Communication Trust

- The Dyslexia SpLD Trust

- The National Sensory Impairment Partnership

Using these resources and thinking about a CYPn you are familiar with, address the following questions.

- How would the information these websites provide contribute towards the delivery of provision to meet the CYPn's assessed needs?

- What are the implications of this additional information in carrying out planned support?

Review

This stage of the assess, plan, do, review cycle ensures that a review is made of the impact of intervention and the quality of the support offered. It evaluates the progress made by the CYPn and addresses how far outcomes have been met. The review should be carried out with the CYPn and their parents. This review allows for the refining and revising of a shared understanding of the CYPn's SEN and the identification of which actions can cease, which should continue and which should change.

Measuring progress and attainment, especially for those CnYP with SEN who typically make much smaller steps of progress, enables interventions to be finely tuned. The challenge for external agencies working with schools is that every education data system is potentially different, making it much harder to compare from one setting to another and ascertain the rate of progress that an individual is making against that of their peers.

In assessing the small steps of progress CnYP might take, especially where they have significant SEN, the Performance scale (P scale) has been used (DfE, 2017b). The P scale details a set of performance indicators across the curriculum for those CnYP working at below national curriculum (NC) levels in Key Stages 1–4. However, the Rochford Review (Standards and Testing Agency, 2016) recommended that P levels should be replaced by pre-key stage standards in English and mathematics for CnYP working below the standards of NC tests (Standards and Testing Agency, 2018a; Standards and Testing Agency, 2018b). Furthermore, for CnYP who are not engaged in subject specific learning, the Rochford Review endorsed the findings of The Complex Learning Difficulties and Disabilities (CLDD) research project (Specialist Schools and Academies Trust, 2011).

This recommends that early cognitive development and learning should focus on a range of skills that enable CnYP to engage in learning and work towards autonomous learning choices. Key to the development of such skills is the CYPn's engagement in learning activities in seven specific areas. These are:

- awareness;
- curiosity;
- investigation;
- discovery;
- anticipation;
- persistence;
- initiation.

In focusing on these seven areas, the practitioner can then make adaptations to the learning environment. Such adaptations, as well as the CYPn's response to such changes, are recorded in an Engagement Profile and Scale; thus, building a picture of progress as well as effective approaches over time. In this way, a holistic picture of the CYPn becomes evident and encompasses education, health and social aspects of development. Only by such wide-ranging consideration of the capabilities and development potential of the whole person can appropriate planning and action for progress in learning be carried out.

Transition

For a CYPn requiring targeted SEN support, the planning of any transition should ensure that the CYPn's views and wishes are taken into account fully by all practitioners involved and should inform decisions made. Interestingly, when considering transition, the CoP focuses on the processes such as exchange of information rather than the experiences of the CYPn (6.57 and 8.32). Nevertheless, valuable information about the CYPn does need to be transferred from setting to setting and this information transfer should not be reliant upon the parent as messenger. This tendency is a common negative thread in parenting social media forums. Threads in such forums report frustration that services and service systems do not always automatically join up and communicate efficiently. Hence the transition process for the CYPn is not as effective as it might be. From the CYPn's experience this may mean their learning could be compromised, resulting in a detrimental effect on their progress, socially and academically. Where there has been involvement from services other than education in meeting the CYPn's needs, information from these services, such as health and social care, also needs to be communicated to the new setting. This is important whatever the age of the CYPn. A key person involved in providing a bridge between educational settings and different practitioners, is the SENCO.

The role of the SENCO

The role of the SENCO is to provide information and professional guidance to practitioners who work closely with the CYPn and their family to ensure that appropriate support and high quality teaching is delivered.

The CoP identifies that early years providers other than maintained nursery schools are expected to have arrangements in place for meeting children's SEN. Many LAs make use of an Area SENCO to provide advice and guidance and to make links between education, health and social care to facilitate appropriate early provision and to aid transition to compulsory schooling.

Maintained nursery schools as well as primary and secondary settings **must** identify a qualified teacher to be the SENCO (CoP, 6.85). Since 2009, a teacher taking on the role of SENCO is required to undertake a mandatory postgraduate qualification within 3 years of taking up the post (Department for Children, Schools and Families, 2008). The SENCO will provide leadership and professional guidance within their setting. They are responsible for the day-to-day operation of SEN policy and for co-ordinating the specific provision made for individual CnYP with SEN. The CoP (6.87) recommends that for the SENCO to be most effective, they should be a member of the senior leadership team. They should also be involved in the regular review of the expertise and resources used to provide for children with SEN, alongside school improvement approaches. Similarly, the CoP (6.3) identifies that a member of the governing body should be given specific responsibility for the oversight of SEN provision within the school.

It is noteworthy that the 2019 House of Commons Education Committee SEND report (House of Commons, 2019a) has recommended that SENCOs should complete the mandatory qualification upon taking up the role and has also emphasised the importance of ongoing SENCO continuous professional development (CPD). This strongly worded report recognises that a system is only as strong as the practitioners working within it and identifies the vital expert role SENCOs provide.

FE providers should ensure that they name a person who has oversight of the SEN provision. However, there is no obligation for them to hold the mandatory SENCO qualification, unlike in schools. The expectation is that they would contribute to both the strategic and operational management of the college (CoP, 7.22).

CRITICAL QUESTIONS

Using the information from the CoP above, it is evident that all educational establishments should have a designated person overseeing the provision for CnYP with SEN.

- Given that the requirements for the designated person for SEN within the three age phases differ, identify the reasons for this.

- How do you think this difference of requirement might impact upon the CYPn's journey through their education?

The SENCO's consultancy and strategic role is pivotal in ensuring that all parties are provided with opportunities to discuss and share information. This might take place, for example, within a multi-agency meeting or Team Around the Child (TAC) or Team Around the Family (TAF) meeting. The SENCO should ensure that all planning is personalised and takes the views of the CYPn and their family into account. In addition to enabling the CYPn and their family to share their views, the associated record keeping might take the form of an individual provision map, a one-page profile, a pupil passport or other person-centred thinking tools. The SENCO is also tasked with managing the provision and resource for multiple CnYP across the setting and must make strategic decisions about what **must**, should and could be provided within budgetary and staffing constraints (CoP, 6.90).

Within the four broad areas of SEN, some CnYP will require the ongoing involvement of specialist services across health and social care, such as physiotherapists, epilepsy nurses or children's disability teams. It is the responsibility of the SENCO to co-ordinate this provision. Many of these CnYP will be able to have their SEN met effectively within their local community mainstream setting as a result of the involvement of specialists.

Involvement of specialists

The CoP states that where a CYPn continues to make less than expected progress, despite evidence-based support and interventions that are matched to the CYPn's area of need, the education setting should consider involving specialists. Such specialists can be involved at any age or stage from early years to FE (CoP, 5.9; 6.58–6.62; 7.22–7.33). They may be employed by the setting itself or come from outside agencies, such as education, health and social care services operating within the local area, or from the private and voluntary sector. The purpose of engaging specialist services is to secure additional knowledge and understanding of the CYPn and their SEN in a specific area. Some specialist services will be free at the point of service, some traded services may make a charge, typically to the education setting. Parents may also seek to secure privately commissioned specialist support such as educational psychology assessments, sensory assessments etc.

However, it must be recognised that several potential barriers may present themselves in the process of working with specialists. These might include differences in working practice in terms of referral pathways, criteria and thresholds; differences in terminology, service capacity and flexibility; and, for many services, that they now operate through a traded offer that must be purchased by the setting. The implementation of the General Data Protection Regulation (GDPR) (Data Protection Act, 2018) has resulted in a slowing of information sharing while new systems are put in place, as health and LA services are required to identify and agree secure methods of communicating CnYP's information.

Anecdotal evidence suggests that LAs have overseen a significant decline in services available to support CnYP with lower levels of SEN need. These include specialist services that support pupils with high-incidence needs such as dyslexia, autism and social emotional and mental health needs, as they seek to make savings and focus on their statutory duties.

CRITICAL QUESTIONS

When more than one specialist service is involved, it is important not to lose sight of a holistic view of the CYPn. When thinking about a YPn in an FE setting consider the following questions.

*   What specialist service is best placed to identify the primary SEN need?

*   If the education setting does not provide this categorisation and data, who should?

*   How do you ensure that the YPn is seen and understood as a whole person?

*   How can you make sure that the implication of the GDPR does not hinder the effective transfer of information to those whose understanding and actions will be influenced by access to appropriate information?

Evidence-based practice for effective SEN support

As previously identified, when selecting interventions to meet outcomes, it is important to ensure there is reliable evidence of effectiveness. Research carried out on behalf of the DfE (2017a) resulted in a SEN support toolkit and a partner guide for senior leaders in education settings. These aim to enable school leaders and SENCOs to make informed choices particularly within a climate of diminishing financial resource.

As a result of this research work, seven key features are identified that demonstrate effective SEN support.

They can be summarised as:

*   Culture, leadership and management
    *   The school ethos and vision demonstrate a commitment to inclusion whereby CnYP with SEN are valued and positively reflected within the school community.

*   High quality teaching
    *   Staff can identify barriers to learning, match needs to appropriate support and effectively monitor and review progress.
    *   Staff take responsibility for all CnYP's progress and are skilled at adapting and differentiating their teaching.

*   Use of expertise
    *   Access to CPD which addresses both theory and practice.
    *   Clear processes for how and when to work with specialists.
    *   Use of the SENCO strategically, and as a consultant.

- Personalisation

  – Individual tailored or bespoke packages of support that address the full range of CnYP's needs.

  – High expectations for progress, achievement and outcomes; the development of independence; an understanding of and celebration of strengths and successes.

  – CnYP and families are treated as partners with respect and their contributions are valued.

- Flexible use of evidence-based strategies

  – Minimal withdrawal from and disruption to mainstream learning.

- Progress tracking

  – Regular data collection to facilitate early identification.

  – Progress is monitored to underpin decision-making with clear systems of accountability.

- Communication and collaboration

  – Open and transparent information sharing that creates trusted and supportive relationships, with everyone focused on the same goals.

Although research and evidence-based approaches identify the ways in which needs at SEN support can be better met, it must be recognised that individual education settings and multi-academy trusts (MATs) will support CnYP in diverse ways, making it challenging for CnYP and parents to navigate the system.

One of the most common approaches within targeted provision is the use of TAs. The DISS project (Blatchford et al, 2009) found that many TAs had a direct teaching role, interacting daily both one to one and in small groups and often with CnYP with learning and behaviour needs. Further evidence from the Education Endowment Foundation (EEF) through the Effective Deployment of Teaching Assistants (EDTA) Project (Webster et al, 2013) showed that TAs spent the majority of their time supporting CnYP with the most need. Although the effective use of TAs can contribute towards CnYP's progress, cuts to school funding have been identified as being one factor in reducing the number of TAs and support staff.

The role of funding

In order to consider the fulfilment of a CYPn's aspirations, the whole area of funding is brought into play. All mainstream schools and academies are provided with funding, which is determined by a local funding formula. A non-ring-fenced 'notional SEN budget' (CoP, 6.96) is made available for the school to provide high quality support using the whole of the budget. It is the responsibility of the headteacher and SENCO to plan their normal budget considering what their approach is to meeting the needs of CnYP with SEN. Schools are expected to provide support costing up to a nationally prescribed threshold per pupil per year, but for CnYP who may require more expensive provision, the LA should provide additional funding.

CnYP in specific circumstances

While the CoP Chapter 10 recognises that there are CnYP in specific circumstances who require additional consideration, it must not be assumed that they have a SEN. If SEN are identified, then provision which is '*different from or additional to*' (CoP, 6.15) is put into place. This provision may mean targeted support for a brief or longer period of time and must consider the CYPn holistically. Some CnYP in specific circumstances, like any other CYPn, may require bespoke provision, while yet other CnYP may benefit from an EHC plan. We discuss the more particular nature of provision for different groups of CnYP in specific circumstances in Chapter 6 and Part three. Such provision often has implications for practitioners beyond the educational setting the CYPn attends.

There is comprehensive guidance within Chapter 10 of the CoP regarding CnYP in specific circumstances. This chapter is an addition to the 2014 CoP. For such CnYP to achieve good outcomes they require effective joined-up service provision. It is important to recognise that groups of CnYP in specific circumstances include groups of CnYP you may not have thought about or experienced working with as a practitioner. These groups are identified in Chapter 10 of the CoP and include:

* looked-after children (CoP, 10.1–10.11);

* care leavers (CoP, 10.12);

* CnYP with SEN and social care needs, including children in need (CoP, 10.13–10.25);

* CnYP educated out of area (CoP, 10.26–10.29);

* CnYP with SEN who are educated at home (CoP, 10.30–10.18);

* CnYP in alternative provision (CoP, 10.39–20.46);

* CnYP with SEN and who are in hospital (CoP, 10.47–10.52);

* children of service personnel (CoP, 10.53–10.54);

* CnYP in youth custody (CoP, 10.55–10.56 and 10.60–10.150).

While it is vital for all practitioners involved in working with CnYP in specific circumstances to strive together to enable good outcomes, inevitably for some CnYP disagreement occurs about how this might be achieved. This may be the case for any CYPn, whether in specific circumstances or not. It is important therefore to take steps to address disagreement as soon as possible in order to bring effective resolution.

Resolving disagreement

Where a CYPn is considered to have SEN, decisions concerning their provision should be made as soon as possible. Appropriate services, as well as the CYPn and their parents, should work together through open and honest dialogue to agree on the provision to be made. It is this good, open communication which is vital in developing and maintaining relationships of trust between all parties and particularly between parents and educational settings. However, disagreement may arise as a result of different practitioner perspectives and understanding, therefore the SENCO should seek to resolve any disagreement through informal mediation, navigating through the differences in practitioner culture, ethos and processes. This may take many forms such as regular meetings, home visits, telephone calls or emails.

CnYP and their parents can access support from their local independent SENDIASS in this process. Their arrangements cover all CnYP with SEN regardless of whether they have been assessed for or have an EHC plan. Where agreement cannot be found, it is vital that an early resolution of disagreements is sought. Wright et al (2011) focus on the need for early resolution/intervention to prevent disputes from escalating into something more serious and adversarial, possibly via the court process.

Conclusion

This chapter has explored the first stages of SEN support. It has identified that it is a fluid model that involves an increasing number of practitioners. The SENCO's role is paramount in ensuring that the CYPn's SEN are clearly identified and understood. They co-ordinate targeted provision through the assess, plan, do, review cycle by deploying appropriate staffing and resources. The review stage should result in agreed decisions. This may identify the need for bespoke provision. This is examined in Chapter 6.

Further reading and web-based materials

This paper comes out of the doctoral studies of Nick Hodge and Katherine Runswick-Cole. It examines the parent–professional partnership and makes recommendations regarding the empowerment and enabling of effective relationships.

Hodge, N and Runswick-Cole, K (2008) Problematising Parent–Professional Partnerships in Education. *Disability & Society*, 23(6): 236–47.

All of these websites provide specific information and advice to support families and CnYP who have been identified as having one or more of these SEN. Local information and support can be found on the LO for the area where you live.

The Autism Education Trust for CnYP on the autism spectrum: www.autismeducationtrust. org.uk/ (accessed 6 July 2019).

The Communications Trust for speech, language and communication difficulties: www. thecommunicationtrust.org.uk/ (accessed 6 July 2019).

The Dyslexia SpLD Trust on dyslexia and literacy difficulties: www.thedyslexia-spldtrust. org.uk/ (accessed 6 July 2019).

The National Sensory Impairment Partnership for vision impairment, hearing impairment and multisensory impairment: www.natsip.org.uk/ (accessed 6 July 2019).

6 Extending support: bespoke provision

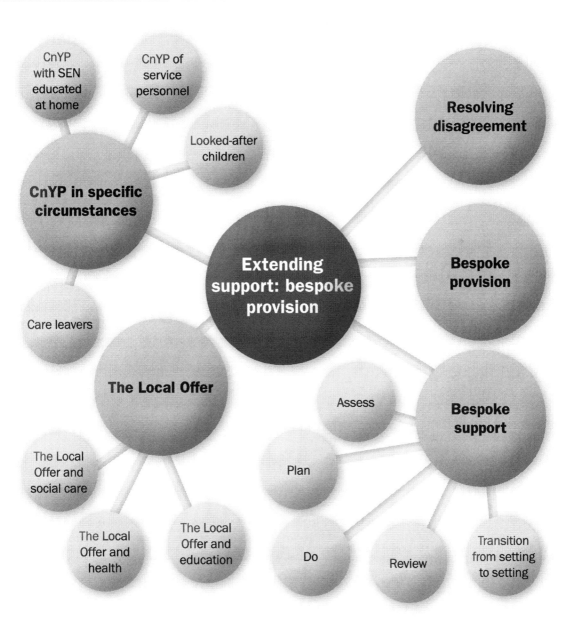

This chapter provides:

- an understanding of bespoke support beyond universal provision and targeted support;
- an examination of specific groups of CnYP;
- an understanding of how the LO supports bespoke provision;
- an understanding of effective transition planning;
- an understanding of how to resolve disagreement.

Bespoke provision

In Chapters 4 and 5, we outlined how the four-part cycle of assess, plan, do, review (graduated approach) provides the means whereby CnYP's progress can be responded to by the relevant practitioners from education, health and social care. For a small number of CnYP the complexity of their need requires individual provision that is specifically tailored in order for progress to be made. Such CnYP will not have an EHC plan but will receive bespoke intervention. This may be short term or extend throughout the CYPn's education.

It is crucial that all such practitioners work together to provide holistic support for CnYP. Additionally, joint commissioning arrangements for education, health and social care should provide ways in which appropriate arrangements for CnYP can be decided and secured at both strategic and service level. Lindsay (2018, p 371) outlines the importance of agreed values and aims between services, including voluntary and community sectors, along with sufficient resources and 'organisational strength' to achieve such aims. Furthermore, he acknowledges that for joined-up thinking to occur between practitioners, there needs to be an understanding of and sympathy for the different ways in which children's needs are conceptualised (Lindsay, 2018, p 373).

Bespoke support

The House of Commons Education Committee SEND report identified that SEN support 'has been a neglected area of focus since 2014' (House of Commons, 2019a, p 16). It has made a number of robust recommendations to address this, all of which are designed to ensure the accountability of all partners involved.

Many CnYP can be adequately supported to make progress in mainstream education. While it is possible that some CnYP may on occasions require bespoke interventions or may benefit from advice and support from health or social care, as stated earlier, such interventions may not be long term. It is important to note that specialist practitioners may work with a CYPn or provide advice to practitioners regardless of whether the CYPn is receiving provision at universal level, or at SEN support (targeted interventions or bespoke provision). As Lindsay (2018, p 372) comments, there is '*a good case for involvement by speech and language therapists, educational psychologists, community paediatricians and others to work at the universal level to aid prevention, as well as to use their expertise with individual children at specialist level*'.

Engaging with a range of different practitioners in order to make the best provision for CnYP demands a willingness from all involved to overcome any potential barriers to working together, such as different professional cultures, expectations, processes and language. Frost (2005) identifies four levels of partnership related to inter-service working. These are:

- level 1, co-operation – services work together towards consistent goals and complementary services, while maintaining their independence;

- level 2, collaboration – services plan together and address issues of overlap, duplication and gaps in service provision towards common outcomes;

- level 3, co-ordination – services work together in a planned and systematic manner towards shared and agreed goals;

- level 4, merger/integration – different services become one organisation in order to enhance service delivery.

If bespoke support that involves a range of different services is to be effective, then it is important that these services work together for the highest level of partnership possible. The culture and working practices of their own profession are adapted in order to empower CnYP and their parents to achieve their aspirations.

In order to make provision that is truly bespoke, the voice of the CYPn in receipt of such support is vital. The UN Convention on the Rights of the Child (United Nations, 1989) states that '*every child has the right to express their views, feelings and wishes in all matters affecting them, and to have their views considered and taken seriously*' (article 12). This demonstrates that it is important to not only give the CYPn a voice, but to take it into account as part of the decision-making process. As the date of this convention shows, this is not a new idea and yet anecdotal evidence suggests that this is yet to be fully embedded with all services, all practitioners and all CnYP and their parents.

Roger Hart (1992) built on the principles in article 12 of the Convention on the Rights of the Child (United Nations, 1989) and developed a conceptual model of participation represented as a ladder. He defines participation as '*the process of sharing decisions which affect one's life and the life of the community in which one lives … Participation is the fundamental right of citizenship*' (Hart, 1992, p 5). Hart's ladder of participation identifies eight levels as seen in Figure 6.1.

Levels of the ladder	Explanation	Degree of participation
8. Child initiated, shared decisions with adults	A supportive environment where CnYP choose to include adults in the decision-making processes	
7. Child initiated and directed	A supportive environment with adults who do not interfere or direct	
6. Adult initiated shared decisions with children	Adult initiated but the decision-making process is shared with CnYP	True partnership
5. Consulted and informed	Adult led, but CnYP understand the process and their opinions are taken seriously	
4. Assigned but informed	Adult led, but CnYP understand the process they are invited to be involved in and have a meaningful role	Participatory partnership
3. Tokenism	Where CnYP are given a voice but have little or no choice about what or how it is communicated and little or no choice to develop their own opinion	
2. Decoration	Adults using children to bolster their case eg the wearing of T shirts for a cause when the CYPn does not know or understand what the cause is about	
1. Manipulation	CnYP's ideas subject to significant influence by adults, yet presented as if they were the CYPn's own	No partnership

Figure 6.1 *Adapted from Hart's ladder of participation (1992)*

Shier (2001) takes Hart's model further and develops a five-stage model of pathways to participation. His model ignores levels 1–3 of Hart's ladder as they are not considered to be participation. Shier identifies five levels of participation.

1.   CnYP are listened to. This is child initiated, but if the CYPn does not volunteer a view, their perspective is not sought.

2.   CnYP are supported in expressing their view. Adults take positive action to encourage CnYP to express their view openly and confidently.

3.   CnYP's views are considered. Adults take CnYP's views seriously and the decisions made are influenced by these views. It is not until this level that the expectation of article 12 of the UN Convention on the Rights of the Child (United Nations, 1989) is met.

4. CnYP are involved in the decision-making process. CnYP are directly involved at the point where decisions are made.

5. CnYP share power and responsibility for decision-making. This demands an explicit commitment on the part of adults to give away some of their power to CnYP.

SCENARIO

Marcus is 11 years old. He has a diagnosis of autism. His primary school have managed his needs through bespoke support. Marcus is due to move to secondary school for the next academic year. He is known to social care as his mum is an alcoholic and his dad works night shifts leaving Marcus vulnerable in terms of care. A meeting has been arranged in order to discuss Marcus' transition to secondary school. Those invited to the meeting are the SENCO from both the primary and the secondary school, Marcus, his parents, the educational psychologist (EP), his social worker and a member of the Autism Assessment Team (health).

CRITICAL QUESTIONS

From the perspectives of one of these participants and using either Hart's or Shier's model of participation, consider the following.

• What level of participation do you think is achievable for Marcus in this transition meeting? Why?

• What would you do to enable Marcus to participate?

• What would need to happen for Marcus to be able to participate at the next level?

• Thinking about any meetings you may have attended previously, what level of participation do you think is most often seen in these meetings? Why is this?

• How far do you think Hart's levels of participation 6–8 (true partnership) are possible in making decisions related to the provision for CnYP such as Marcus? Justify your response.

Assess

For a CYPn to receive bespoke support, they will already have experienced the assess, plan, do, review process and received differentiated teaching and/or intervention at both the universal and targeted stages of provision. This means the needs of the CYPn should be known to all relevant practitioners, with additional advice sought from specialists as appropriate.

As already outlined in Chapter 4, if a child is considered to have SEN or a disability prior to starting school, HPs must inform the parents and involve the LA. Health bodies must also give information to parents about where additional advice can be found, particularly in relation to education and any voluntary organisations that may provide support or advice. Similarly, if a CYPn has been assessed as having social care needs, educational settings including early years providers and colleges should be provided with a contact for social care advice. If there is no health or social care practitioner (SCP) already involved with the CYPn within the educational setting, the SENCO should contact the relevant service for advice or specialist assessments if required. The SENCO must however seek the parents' permission (CoP, 6.59).

When teachers carry out assessments with CnYP it is important to understand that such assessments are in order to make relevant provision for a child, not to make a diagnosis. It can be tempting for teachers to consider a CYPn showing certain behaviours or learning patterns to have autism for example, or dyslexia or other learning differences they are familiar with. If it is considered important to pursue a diagnosis, then this must be carried out by an appropriate practitioner holding appropriate qualifications, such as a medical practitioner, therapist or EP. Lindsay (2018, p 373) considers that a diagnosis is '*potentially helpful*' if it leads to guidance for action.

Regardless of whether a diagnosis is being sought, it is the SENCO's responsibility to engage with practitioners from other services and to strive towards effective partnership. Similarly, those who work with CnYP should do so in a way that encourages their maximum participation.

Plan

In order to make planning effective and tailor-made for the CnYP, it is vital that the outcomes of assessments as well as advice from specialist practitioners should be considered fully. It goes without saying that this holds true for the perspectives of CnYP and parents also. Where a CYPn has a medical condition, it is vital for HPs, schools and colleges to work together to provide ways in which effective support can be offered. This may include the implementation of an HCP as discussed in Chapter 4. It is important not to assume that a CYPn with an HCP also has SEN. For example, a CYPn's inability to use spoken language for communication does not necessarily mean their cognitive function is impaired. Cognitive function should be determined by an EP or other appropriately trained practitioner.

The 2015 CoP (7.37–7.38) states that even from the earliest years, as part of the planning process, attention should be given to preparation for adulthood for CnYP with SEN. In order to work towards this transition, health and SCPs are tasked with understanding the interests, strengths and aspirations of CnYP and using these to secure relevant and individualised outcomes.

Do

Teachers who hold specialist qualifications, for example, in autism, or literacy and dyslexia, or who are specialist leaders in education, may be involved in directly supporting CnYP in schools. Other teachers will hold mandatory qualifications to support CnYP with hearing or vision impairments and multisensory impairments. Additionally, a range of therapists such as physiotherapists, OTs or practitioners from CAMHS may be involved in providing individual support for the child or in giving advice to education settings. These practitioners are expected to work with the SENCO and class/subject teachers in making sure appropriate equipment, strategies and interventions are put in place within the learning environment. Details of bespoke provision within educational settings, such as adult support as well as teaching strategies and approaches, should be recorded on the information system of the setting. Additionally, all provision should be delivered by skilled and knowledgeable staff using programmes and approaches known to be effective (CoP, 6.50).

As already stated, a wide range of health and/or SCPs may be involved in supporting such CnYP and their families. In some cases, school nurses or other practitioners such as those in social care may be asked to act as a key worker for such CnYP. Godson (2014) considers that the role of the key worker is to provide emotional and practical support and to empower the CYPn and/or their parents in making decisions about appropriate provision. This may include the co-ordination of all the services involved with the CYPn and providing advocacy where appropriate.

Review

Reviews for CnYP who are receiving individual support should involve all those who have been working with the CYPn and who know them. While it may not be possible for all parties involved to be present at such reviews, it is essential that they are able to have their views represented. As part of preparation for adulthood from Year 9 onwards (YP aged 13–14), schools are required to extend the partnerships they are developing, to include employment services, businesses, housing agencies, disability and recreation groups. If a YP is attending college, a discussion should take place with the YP to assess the impact and success of their support. There should also be discussion about the YP's future, including what they wish to achieve and how this can be realised. For some YP, it will be appropriate for the college to provide an '*independent skilled supporter*' (CoP, 8.18) to enable them to express their views about their future, including greater autonomy and independence. It is the responsibility of the LA to ensure access to this support.

Hodkinson and Burch (2019) challenge the notion of *support* to gain what they consider are externally imposed ideas and beliefs on the CYPn, such as the desire for employment. They note that the aspirations of CnYP are subject to the agreement of practitioners; however, according to the CoP, such aspirations should promote independent living, employment, good health and community participation (CoP, 7.13). Thus, while CnYP are to be *supported* to express their aspirations, according to Hodkinson and Burch (2019, p 164), this support is '*constrained, curtailed and limited in its outlook*' and attempts to control, coercing CnYP into '*conformity, servitude and normalcy*'.

CRITICAL QUESTIONS

- How much do practitioners feel they are obliged to encourage a CYPn to conform to externally imposed ideas and beliefs, such as the desire for employment, even when this does not coincide with the CYPn's own aspirations?

- How far do parents/CnYP think they have freedom to express their aspirations and be confident all parties can work towards them?

- How do practitioners accept such aspirations and how much do they think they need to adjust aspirations to what might seem more realistic from their perspective?

Transition from setting to setting

Periods of transition occur at key points during a CYPn's educational and life journey; these may coincide with transfer from one age phase to another or into employment and independent living. Nasen (2014) identifies that, at whatever age, these are often very stressful points, while Robinson et al (2018) recognise that in order to achieve a good transition there may be many barriers to overcome. In this chapter, we explore transition points between educational settings. Transitions into employment and independent living are discussed in Part three.

A lot of time and investment is needed by all the relevant stakeholders to ensure transition is smooth and effective. This may include a review of the SEN support or EHC plan. From Year 9, the LA **must** ensure post-16 options are discussed and a tailor-made study programme agreed as required. It is vital that if the YP wishes to attend a different setting, the receiving setting should have access to relevant information from the current setting to aid a smooth transition. However, parents and the YP should agree about the information to be shared, particularly if the YP would like the opportunity to make a fresh start (CoP, 5.47, 6.57, 8.22).

Some YP with SEN may be able to secure a place in higher education. It is the responsibility of the LA, through the LO, to ensure the YP is aware of the support that is available to them and how to access funding through the Disabled Students' Allowance (DSA) in order to support any additional needs during their course (CoP, 8.43–45). Again, it is important to stress that a smooth transition should occur, and where a YP with an EHC plan requests it, a copy of their EHC plan **must** be given to the relevant person within higher education by the LA (CoP, 8.46*).

The Local Offer

Lamb (2015, p74) considers that the importance of the LO has been '*underestimated*' and that it requires '*in strategy and behaviour a far greater shift in thinking than the proposals around the flagship EHC plan*'. This statement concurs with our experience, as practitioners seem to have a greater awareness and knowledge of EHC plans than they do of the information and services available through the LO. However, the LO involves provision from across education, health and social care and covers support and services for the 97 per cent of CnYP who are receiving support through universal, targeted support or specialist, individual provision. It covers providers of early years education, pupil referral units, maintained and non-maintained schools, including special schools, as well as post-16 providers, and seeks to take more account of service users (CoP, 4.32). In many cases it seems to be an untapped resource for practitioners, CnYP and their parents alike.

The Local Offer and education

Each area's LO **must** provide information about the LA's funding arrangements for CnYP with SEN. It must make clear what the arrangements are for securing services and equipment, as well as how CnYP can be supported as they move from one phase of education to another or into adulthood (CoP, 4.32). This is of fundamental importance for CnYP who are receiving bespoke provision. Other information the LA **must** provide regarding educational provision includes:

- teaching approaches, adaptations to the learning environment and curriculum;

- how to access available facilities such as ancillary aids and assistive technology such as supportive communication aids;

- how CnYP's progress is assessed and reviewed, including working with parents and YP;

- how education practitioners are equipped to support CnYP with SEN in their setting, including the practitioner knowing about the need, knowing how to adapt teaching and learning to meet the need and specialist support for staff working with CnYP with SEN;

- how the effectiveness of the provision for CnYP is assessed and monitored;

- what activities, including extra-curricular activities, are available;

- how the social, emotional and mental health of CnYP with SEN is supported.

These arrangements also apply for CnYP who are looked after by the LA (CoP, 4.32).

Additionally, the LA **must** publish childcare options for CnYP with SEN (CoP, 4.38). These include:

- free early education places;

- services from other agencies such as health visitors, Portage and Early Support;

- arrangements for identifying and assessing need as well as reviewing progress including health and development checks;

- support available for parents at home.

The Local Offer and health

The LO **must** include information about what health services are available to CnYP as a result of the JSNA (CoP, 4.40). These include:

• services available from early years to post-16 institutions for children with medical conditions;

• therapies such as physiotherapy, speech and language therapy and mental health services;

• wheelchair services, community equipment, continence service and children's community nursing;

• palliative and respite care;

• support for CnYP when moving between health care services for children to health care services for adults.

The Local Offer and social care

The LO **must** include information about what social care services and other provision are available to CnYP (CoP, 4.32). These include:

• childcare;

• leisure activities;

• support for CnYP when moving between social care services for children to social care services for adults;

• support for YP living independently.

LAs are required by law to provide information on the adult care system, what local provision is offered, how to access it and advice relating to finances (CoP, 4.43). Additionally, a range of short breaks for disabled CnYP and their families should be provided, which should be responsive to local need and reviewed regularly (CoP, 4.44). Furthermore, the LO must give details of support groups available to the parents of CnYP with SEN (CoP, 4.45).

As illustrated above, the LO is a vital source of information, support and resources for all services as well as CnYP and their parents. In the following section, we discuss the particular needs and requirements of some CnYP in specific circumstances, many of whom will access support from education, health and social care and for whom effective partnership between such services is crucial.

CnYP in specific circumstances

Chapter 10 of the CoP clearly identifies particular groups of CnYP who require additional consideration. We list these in Chapter 5. As with any CYPn with SEN, CnYP in specific circumstances with SEN may have their needs met through universal or targeted support, but for some of them a more individually tailored approach may be required. In this next section we consider the implications of this more bespoke provision for four groups of CnYP in specific circumstances.

Looked-after children

CnYP who are being taken into care by the LA are considered to be looked after. This is a legal definition. LAs are required to act as a '*corporate parent*' to such children and **must** treat the CYPn's welfare as paramount (CoP, 10.2). CnYP who are on remand to youth detention accommodation are also considered to be looked after.

The CoP states that about 70 per cent of looked-after children may have some form of SEN and while not all of them will need to have their needs met through bespoke provision, the CoP outlines that a '*significant proportion*' of them will have an EHC plan (CoP, 10.1). The LA **must** be concerned with the educational achievement of looked-after children, no matter where they are placed. There **must** be a designated teacher (DT) for looked-after children in all maintained schools, academies and free schools. This role is different from the one carried out by the SENCO. However, the DT and SENCO should work together closely to enable all staff in the educational setting to understand the implications for the CnYP of being looked after and having SEN.

There is a legal duty, through the Children and Families Act 2014, for a LA officer to be appointed to head up a team of people who will track the progress of looked-after CnYP. Such CnYP are considered to be members of a single, virtual school. Other practitioners, such as social workers and specialist teachers, should work closely with the staff of the virtual school to ensure an effective, joined-up approach.

CnYP who are being looked after by the LA will have a Care Plan (CP) which addresses how their developmental needs should be met. These include health, education, emotional and behavioural development, identity, family and social relationships as well as self-care skills. Within the remit of the CP are the legally required personal education plan (PEP) and the HCP, which will set out what the CYPn's education and health needs are. The assessments for these plans may lead to the identification of SEN. The CoP categorically states that SEN practitioners and all other practitioners involved in the life of the CYPn who is looked after **must** work closely together (CoP, 10.7). The CYPn themselves, their carers and where appropriate their parents, must also be involved. This is especially vital if an EHC plan is being considered (CoP, 10.1–10.11).

SCENARIO

Consider Alfie who featured in Chapter 2.

Alfie is 5 years old. He lives with foster parents. This is his third set of foster parents. He can have violent outbursts at school if other children don't play with him in the way he chooses; consequently, he does not have many friends. He has a short concentration span and is not working to expected levels in the classroom. Alfie's aspiration is to be a superhero with superpowers. The SENCO has asked the LA to carry out an assessment of his needs.

IMPLICATIONS FOR PRACTICE

Adopting the role of a social worker and using the relevant sections of Chapter 10 of the CoP, answer the following questions.

- What are the timelines for assessment for Alfie?

- What sources of information might you access in order to provide a relevant contribution to the assessment process?

- Who might you liaise with and why?

Care leavers

The age at which a CYPn is no longer looked after by the LA can vary. Some CnYP leave care at 16 or 17, while others continue to be looked after until they are 18. Some YP in long-term foster placements may remain living with their foster parents after their 18th birthday, but they are no longer considered to be looked after. LAs are required to provide a personal adviser (PA) who is responsible for providing advice and signposting relevant services. A Pathway Plan (PP) should be prepared, which supports care leavers as they transition from care to adulthood until the age of 25 or employment (CoP, 10.12).

CnYP with SEN educated at home

Provision is made within the Education Act 1996 for CnYP to have the right to be educated at home. This includes CnYP with SEN. While some parents may elect to educate their CYPn at home because of their own convictions and philosophy of education, other parents may feel that the SEN support being made available at school is not sufficient to meet their needs. As a result, they decide to educate their CYPn at home. This education '*must be suitable to the child's age, ability, aptitude and SEN*' (CoP, 10.30). Where the CYPn's SEN is already known to the LA, they should work in partnership with parents to ensure the needs of the CYPn are met, including the use of funding where appropriate. While LAs should support the education of CnYP being educated at home, they do not have the right to enter the family home to check on the appropriateness of the education being provided. YP being educated at home may receive education until the age of 18 in order to meet the requirement for them to be involved in education and training until adulthood.

Parents choosing to educate their CYPn at home must notify the school where the CYPn is registered to inform them in writing that the CYPn is receiving education elsewhere and not at the school. The school **must** then remove the CYPn's name from their admissions register. However, if the school is a special school, then the CYPn's name can only be removed with the consent of the LA. All parents, and especially those dissatisfied with the SEN provision in the education setting, should be given information about the right to request an EHC needs assessment as well as the right to appeal (CoP, 10.30–10.38).

CnYP of service personnel

It is recognised in the CoP that CnYP whose parents are service personnel may face difficulties which are unique to them due to their parents' employment. Parents employed in the services may relocate more frequently than others leading to constant change for families, and for CnYP with SEN a potential delay in assessment and provision. Additionally, the CnYP of service personnel may experience anxiety or emotional difficulties due to changes of their social environment, their educational setting, separation from family members and the deployment of family in areas of risk or danger (CoP, 10.54). The Ministry of Defence (MOD) provides an advisory service, the Children's Education Advisory Service (CEAS), to give guidance to service parents, education settings and LAs. This includes advice and support about SEN. Some CnYP of service personnel may be able to be educated in mainstream schools in overseas locations. This is provided by Service Children's Education (SCE).

The CoP (10.55) makes it clear that CnYP of service personnel should not be disadvantaged because of the lifestyle they lead due to their parents' employment. This has implications for all practitioners involved with such CnYP, who should ensure that their own way of working does not impede the educational provision being made. Where CnYP are considered to have SEN, education settings should:

- ensure the efficient and timely transfer of all relevant records between education settings, whether within the UK or overseas;

- ensure that reviews for CnYP with SEN understand that such CnYP could have been to multiple education settings for limited periods of time with the resultant impact on their educational progress;

- ensure that CnYP should have access to assessment and provision based on their educational need regardless of whether their attendance at any particular educational establishment is short term or long term;

- consider how any funding available through the Service Pupils' Premium (SPP) could be effectively used in meeting the needs of CnYP with SEN (CoP, 10.56).

Where there is a service community within the LA area, the commissioning of services from partners such as health and social care should be carefully considered, and the impact of any service-related concerns taken into account. Where an assessment of a CYPn is being carried out, or an EHC plan devised, LAs **must** request advice from CEAS. Where a CYPn moves from one LA to another, the EHC plan should be transferred to the new LA within 15 days from when they become aware of the move. It is then the responsibility of the receiving LA to liaise with the parents to make sure appropriate review arrangements are in place. The receiving LA **must** make sure that the SEN provision set out in the EHC plan is delivered and available as soon as the CYPn arrives in their authority (CoP, 10.53–10.57).

Resolving disagreement

While the CoP stresses the importance of effective partnership working between CnYP, parents and practitioners, it also recognises that there is scope for tensions to occur. It is almost inevitable that at some point during a CYPn's journey into adulthood there will be differences of opinion as to how best to secure progress and how to achieve aspirations. A good starting point when exploring ways of resolving disagreements is to turn to the CoP where Chapter 11 sets out the following key principles.

- Decisions about provision should be made by all interested parties using person-centred approaches with the views of the CYPn being fully considered.
- Open communication between all practitioners to enable full participation of all.
- Providing good, clear information to enable effective decision-making.
- Providing details of disagreement resolution and mediation procedures across education, health and social care.

A concise summary can be found in the CoP at 11.2.

When considering how to resolve differences, it is important to note the terminology. The CoP suggests that *disagreement resolution* and *mediation* are used interchangeably, yet under the Children and Families Act 2014 they are seen as distinct and different processes. LAs must make a disagreement resolution service available to CnYP and parents (CoP, 11.6). This service is voluntary and must be undertaken with agreement from all parties. It should help resolve four main types of disagreement, mainly connected with the performance of duties by agencies including educational settings. These are:

- how a school setting and the LA are carrying out their EHC duties regardless of whether the CYPn has an EHC plan;
- how educational settings including post-16 institutions are providing provision for a specific CYPn;
- between CCGs or LAs regarding health or social care provision;
- between LAs and commissioning bodies.

Gersch et al (1998) suggest an assumption that disagreement and conflict are destructive and there are only two outcomes – win or lose. This is not conducive to working together to secure the best interests of the CYPn, which is one of the guiding principles of the CoP. However, if disagreement cannot be resolved and the mediation process is not effective, then the formal process for resolving disagreement via the Special Educational Needs and Disability Tribunal (SENDIST) may be pursued. This is explored in more detail in Chapter 13.

Conclusion

This chapter has explored how bespoke support can be extended in order to understand fully the needs of CnYP, some of whose circumstances may require additional consideration. This more detailed and holistic understanding may indicate the need for a statutory assessment. Part three addresses this process.

Further reading and web-based materials

This research details some of the approaches that were found to be beneficial for CnYP with SEN in transitioning from school to further/higher education, training, employment or self-employment.

Hanson, J, Codina, G and Neary, S (2017) *Transition Programmes for Young Adults with SEND. What Works?* London: The Careers & Enterprise Company.

This report examines the impact of virtual schools, established by LAs to support and improve the educational achievement of looked-after children. The report draws on evidence from cases and from the views of carers; CnYP; practitioners, including LA managers and social workers; and representatives from schools, colleges and the voluntary sector in nine LAs.

Ofsted (2012) *The Impact of Virtual Schools on the Educational Progress of Looked After Children.* [online] Available at: www.gov.uk/government/publications/the-impact-of-virtual-schools-on-the-education-of-looked-after-children (accessed 30 July 2019).

PART THREE EDUCATION, HEALTH AND CARE PLANS

7 Understanding the EHC assessment process and plan

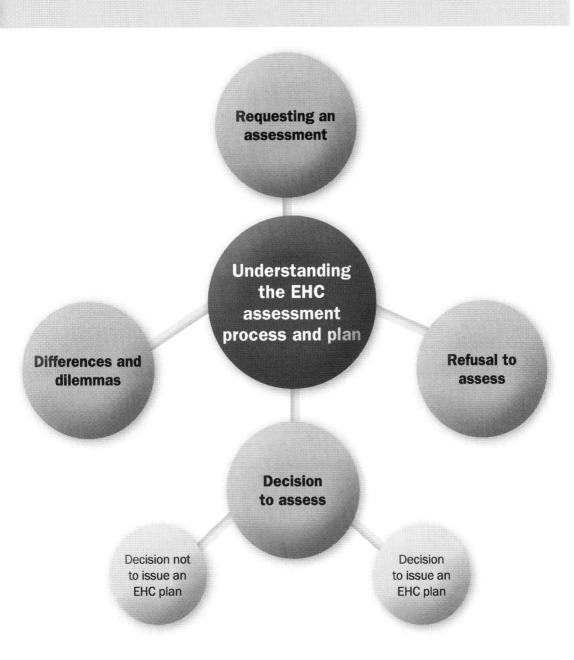

This chapter provides:

- an understanding of how an EHC plan is requested, the assessment process, decision-making and issuing of a plan if agreed;

- implications for all practitioners involved in the process of EHC assessment and planning;

- a discussion about some of the differences and dilemmas related to the EHC process since the 2015 SEND CoP was introduced.

Requesting an assessment

The 2015 SEND CoP clearly identifies '*the general presumption of mainstream education*' (DfE and DH, 2015, 1.38). It also recognises that CnYP with more complex SEN may require an EHC needs assessment. This assessment seeks to determine whether the LA needs to make provision to enable the CYPn to secure the best possible outcomes across education, health and social care, thus preparing them sufficiently for adulthood.

Legislation from the Children and Families Act 2014 states that '*The local authority must secure an EHC needs assessment for a child or young person if, after having regard of any views expressed and evidence submitted … the authority is of the opinion that (a) the child or young person **has or may** have special education needs, <u>and</u> (b) it **may be necessary** for special education provision to be made for a child or young person in accordance with an EHC Plan*' (Section 36(8)) (authors' emphasis).

With the use of the word **may** ambiguity is created as to whether the CYPn has SEN and therefore may require provision. This means that when determining whether a decision to assess is necessary, the legal threshold is low. The implications of this legal test will be discussed later on in this chapter.

Parents, YP over the age of 16, schools, post-16 institutions and others such as HPs and SCPs, probation officers, a youth offending officer or a family friend may request the LA to conduct an assessment (CoP, 9.8). This request should be made with the knowledge and, wherever possible, the agreement of the CYPn or their parent. Once a request is submitted, it triggers the LA legal decision-making process which has two parts. This must comply with a statutory 20 week timescale as illustrated in Table 7.1. It may be possible to complete all statutory processes in fewer than 20 weeks if all information is readily available and if there is no disagreement or undue complexity. It is important to recognise that a request for a statutory assessment may be refused and if the assessment proceeds, it is not guaranteed that this will result in the issuing of an EHC plan.

Table 7.1 *EHC assessment timeline and decision-making process*

Request received 0 weeks to 6 weeks
LA notify (CoP, 9.13): • parent; • health service; • LA officers responsible for social care for CnYP with SEN; • educational setting. Evidence considered (CoP, 9.14): • progress and attainment of CYPn; • nature, extent and context of CYPn's SEN; • a graduated response to need, ie progress made only as a result of much intervention. Decision-making: i) does the CYPn have or may they have SEN **and** ii) is it necessary for SEN provision to be made in accordance with an EHC plan? **Outcomes**: Agree to assess **or** Refuse to assess The LA must give the reason/s for not proceeding, notify parents and other parties, inform parents and YP of rights to appeal (CoP, 9.17–9.19)
Agree to assess 6 weeks to 16 weeks LA seeks views, information and advice from (CoP, 9.49): • parent, using a 'tell it once' approach; • CYPn; • education setting; • health care practitioners; • educational psychologist; • social care practitioners; • services related to provision to assist the YP in preparation for adulthood and independent living (Year 9 onwards); • any person requested by the child's parent or YP, where the LA considers it reasonable to do so. Advice should be provided within 6 weeks of the request. Advice should inform about the CYPn's EHC needs, provision required to meet those identified needs to achieve outcomes and the strategies and support deemed necessary to achieve them.

Outcomes:

Agree to issue an EHC plan; draft plan prepared with the CYPn and parent (CoP, 9.53).

or

Based upon the information submitted, decide an EHC plan is not necessary; that the CYPn's SEN can be met from the resources already available.

The LA must give the reason/s for not proceeding, notify parents and other parties, inform parents and YP of rights to appeal (CoP, 9.57–9.59).

Issue an EHC plan

16 weeks to 20 weeks

- Consideration given to a personal budget.
- Final EHC plan contains SMART (specific, measurable, achievable, realistic, time-bound) long-term targets and should identify arrangements for setting short-term targets. All targets must address identified outcomes including those related to education, health and social care.
- Final EHC plan details education, health and social care provision to meet identified needs.
- Final EHC plan identifies name and type of school/institution to be attended by CYPn.
- Final EHC plan has an identified review date.
- Final EHC plan to be issued no later than 20 weeks.

Refusal to assess

If the LA decision made is not to proceed, LA officers must inform the parent within 6 weeks of the receipt of the original request and must provide reasons for that decision alongside the parents' rights to appeal. This decision is informed by evidence submitted (CoP, 9.14) that demonstrates the ability or otherwise of the educational provider to undertake relevant and purposeful action to enable the CYPn to make progress. Such evidence includes:

- academic attainment and rate of progress;

- the type, level and context of the CYPn's SEN;

- actions taken to meet and remediate need;

- the level of intervention and support provided above what would typically be expected through the education setting's resources;

- the physical, social, emotional development and health needs as understood by health and care practitioners;

- if a YPn is over 18, whether additional time is required to complete their education or training.

Where evidence indicates that the CYPn has or may have SEN and requires provision at a level beyond SEN support, the decision is made to proceed to a full assessment.

Decision to assess

The LA **must** ensure parents and CnYP are provided with the information and support necessary to enable their participation in these decisions (CoP, 9.21). The views, wishes and feelings of CnYP and parents should be expressed as part of the assessment process both in the here and now and looking towards the future, ie in preparation for adulthood. A YPn from 16 years of age who is deemed to have the mental capacity has decision-making rights and should be engaged with directly.

In supporting the assessment process all practitioners should:

- use clear, ordinary language and images;

- highlight the CYPn's strengths and capabilities;

- seek to understand the CYPn's interests, hopes and aspirations;

- tailor support to the individual CYPn;

- organise assessments to minimise demands on families;

- identify outcomes that are appropriate to need, and which will bring about realisation of aspirations.

Additionally, all practitioners **must** respond within 6 weeks to the LA request for information (CoP, 9.52).

The DfE (2017c) commissioned a qualitative investigation of user experiences of the EHC planning process. It identified a number of factors contributing to overall satisfaction in the EHC plan process. They were:

- one individual can make a huge difference;

- access to dedicated specialist support with the EHC assessment process;

- having the EHC plan ready before a transition between settings;

- working together with sustained face-to-face contact between the family and practitioners;

- involving the CYPn in a meaningful manner.

SCENARIO

Sam has a diagnosis of autism. His mum is struggling to get acknowledgement from educational staff in his primary school that his SEN are complex. She considers that an EHC plan is necessary to support his ongoing progress as he moves into the local secondary school. She makes a request to the LA for an EHC assessment, which is agreed.

IMPLICATIONS FOR PRACTICE

From the perspective of your own practice:

• What is your role in providing information, advice and support for Sam and his mum when the EHC assessment is being undertaken?

• How do you ensure that you have sufficient knowledge about EHC processes and plans such that you could identify Sam's strengths and needs within your area of expertise?

• How would you identify how Sam's needs can be appropriately met within a secondary school context?

• How do you collaborate effectively with practitioners from different disciplines to establish a holistic understanding of Sam during the EHC assessment process?

Decision not to issue an EHC plan

If the full range of assessment evidence indicates that the CYPn's needs can be met within a setting's resources, the decision is made not to issue an EHC plan. The LA must notify parents, the YPn, the education setting and the health service, giving the reasons for that decision. Surprisingly this does not include notification to social care (CoP, 9.57) although it would be good practice to inform them if they had involvement with the CYPn. Notification must take place within 16 weeks of the initial request for assessment being submitted. Information about the appeals process, mediation, availability of information, advice and support together with disagreement resolution services must also be provided to the parent and the YPn.

Decision to issue an EHC plan

Using the evidence submitted by all practitioners, LA officers create a draft EHC plan. This is issued to the parents and CYPn for their comments. A further opportunity for parental input is provided at a meeting as part of the collaborative process with practitioners who are actively involved with the CYPn. In our experience, attendance at such meetings is not fully representative of all parties, with health and care colleagues often absent. While each LA will have a locally agreed format for EHC plans, Table 7.2 illustrates the statutory sections that **must** be separately labelled (CoP, 9.69).

Table 7.2 *Statutory sections that must be separately labelled*

Statutory section		Details to be included about the CYPn
(A)	Views, interests and aspirations of the CYPn	Past history, future goals, details of how to communicate effectively to help decision-making
(B)	The CYPn's SEN	Identified SEN, including any health and social care needs
(C)	The CYPn's health needs which relate to their SEN	Health needs identified through the assessment process and that relate specifically to their SEN
(D)	The CYPn's social care needs which relate to their SEN	Social care needs identified through the assessment process and that relate specifically to their SEN. Other social care needs not linked to SEN can be identified, eg child in need or child protection needs
(E)	Outcomes sought for CYPn	Range of outcomes covering education, health and social care, with details of steps needed to achieve them and identified arrangement for monitoring progress
(F)	Special educational provision required by CYPn	Provision to meet need – must be detailed, specific and quantifiable
(G)	Health provision reasonably required by the learning difficulty or disability that result in the CYPn having SEN	Provision that is specific and quantifiable, provides details of who will support and how it relates to the identified outcomes
(H1)	Any social care provision that must be made for a CYPn under 18 resulting from section 2 of the Chronically Sick and Disabled Persons Act (CSDPA) 1970	Provision that is specific and quantifiable, provides details of who will support and how it relates to the identified outcomes – must specify all services required, eg practical assistance and adaptation in the home
(H2)	Social care provision reasonably required by the learning difficulty or disability that results in the CYPn having SEN	Provision that is specific and quantifiable, provides details of who will support and how it relates to the identified outcomes
(I)	Placement	Educational placement or type of placement
(J)	Personal budget	Personal budget that will be used to secure provision and work towards identified outcomes
(K)	Advice and information	All advice and information gathered and relied on must be set out in appendices

The only changes that can be made to a draft plan are those requested by the YPn or parents (CoP, 9.125). If changes cannot be agreed, the final EHC plan can still be issued and parents must be informed of their rights to appeal.

Some parents or YP may request a personal budget to secure provision identified in the EHC plan. A personal budget is an optional source of LA funding used by families to secure special educational, health and social care provision. Personal budgets are discussed in more detail in Chapter 8.

The Children and Families Act 2014 details the parents' and YPn's right to request a particular maintained, non-maintained or independent education setting to be named on their EHC plan. The LA must comply with parental or the YPn's preference and name the school or college in the EHC plan unless:

• *'it would be unsuitable for the age, ability, aptitude or SEN of the child or young person', or*

• *'the attendance of the child or young person there would be incompatible with the efficient education of others, or the efficient use of resources'*

CoP (2015, 9.79)

Where the parent or YPn does not identify a setting or the request for their setting is not met, the LA must specify mainstream provision in the EHC plan.

SCENARIO

Sam has a diagnosis of autism. He now has an EHC plan in preparation for starting secondary school. Mum wants him to attend his local secondary school with his friends. However, the secondary school believes his attendance *'would be incompatible with the efficient education of others, or the efficient use of resources'* (CoP, 9.79).

CRITICAL QUESTIONS

From a parental perspective and referring to reasonable steps (CoP, 9.91–9.94), consider the following.

• What reasons may have contributed to that decision being reached?

• What impact might this decision have upon Sam and yourself?

The final EHC plan, as well as being issued to parents and the CYPn, is issued to the named education setting who **must** admit the CYPn, and to the relevant CCG. All those involved in teaching or supporting the CYPn should be made aware of the CYPn's needs and the provision required to deliver the identified outcomes. A formal review of the EHC plan should take place annually. An early review should be called if the CYPn's SEN change. These review processes are discussed in Chapter 13.

Differences and dilemmas

While every intention is that an EHC plan, when issued, should meet the needs of the CYPn, this raises implications for strategic planning and budget management across education, health and social care at a local, regional and national level.

The DfE England statistics (2019b) demonstrate that the number of EHC plans has increased each year since their introduction in 2014. The areas of largest increase are the 0–5 and 20–25 age groups. This inevitably raises concerns regarding the funding of this provision, with resultant tensions, and presents those making strategic and commissioning decisions with complex dilemmas to address.

The House of Commons Education Committee report (House of Commons, 2019b, p 38) identified that '*schools felt unable—and were perhaps insufficiently willing—to provide a graduated response to additional needs before resorting to statutory support systems*'. Additionally, it was found that a lack of parental confidence in SEN support and schools' inclusive practice were contributory factors in increased requests for EHC plans.

The decisions to both assess and issue a plan are wholly reliant upon the facts presented for each case and the unique and varying circumstances. As we stated earlier, this decision-making requires an understanding of what is meant by *may be necessary*. Case law has reinforced this low threshold. In the 2018 calendar year only 25 per cent of initial requests for assessment were refused. For those cases that go to tribunal, the majority are found in favour of the appellant, ie the parent or YPn (Long and Roberts, 2019).

In a report from the National Association of Headteachers (NAHT), it was identified that the education system is struggling to meet the needs of its most vulnerable pupils. Cuts to health and social care provision resulted in '*teachers at the front line supporting a range of children's needs*' (NAHT, 2018, p 2). Other key findings from respondents were:

- only two per cent of headteachers indicated top up funding was sufficient to meet EHC plans;

- 94 per cent of headteachers find it harder to resource support than previously;

- 83 per cent of headteachers reported not receiving *any* funding from health and social care budgets to support EHC plans;

- 75 per cent of headteachers indicated that practitioners from health and social care rarely attend annual reviews.

The Local Government Association (2018) research raises four particular interlinked and important quandaries and concerns.

1. Demands upon LA high-needs funding stem from increasing numbers of EHC plans and also the rate of permanent exclusions. There is now a growing gap between high-needs funding and high-needs expenditure.

2. Underlying demographic changes: increases in pupil populations, along with advances in medical science, the impact of adverse child experiences, rising levels of poverty and better diagnoses of some conditions.

3. National education policy decisions that do not explicitly incentivise or reward mainstream education settings to be inclusive.

4. The combined impact of constraints placed upon mainstream school budgets, along with budget cuts across the preventative and early intervention support services in education, health and social care. It should also be noted that increased costs in part are rising because CnYP with EHC plans are being educated in ever more specialist forms of provision such as maintained special schools, special academies or independent and non-maintained special schools (INMSS). This has cost an estimated £277 million over 4 years.

While the CoP raises parental expectation, educational settings operate increasingly autonomously. LAs retain sole statutory responsibility for the CYPn yet hold no hard levers. These conflicting agendas may result in irreconcilable tensions.

Conclusion

In this chapter we have examined the process of requesting, assessing for and issuing an EHC plan. We have identified some of the differences and dilemmas, many of which are not addressed in the CoP 2015. Subsequent chapters discuss the EHC plan process from different practitioner perspectives.

Further reading and web-based materials

This is a review making 30 recommendations for school leaders and addressing the disproportionality high numbers of CnYP with SEN who are excluded.

DfE (2019) *Timpson Review of School Exclusion*. [online] Available at: assets.publishing. service.gov.uk/government/uploads/system/uploads/attachment_data/file/ 807862/Timpson_review.pdf (accessed 9 August 2019).

This website provides independent advice and guidance about the EHC plan process.

Independent Provider of Special Education Advice: www.ipsea.org.uk/ehc-needs-assessments (accessed 9 August 2019).

8 The journey of the child or young person and their parent

What CnYP and parents can expect from the assessment and planning process

What CnYP and parents can expect from the LA

YP with SEN who are in youth custody

The journey of the child or young person and their parent

How CnYP and parents contribute to preparing for an EHC plan

CnYP in specific circumstances

The right to request a personal budget

CnYP educated out of area

CnYP with SEN in alternative provision

The resolution of disagreement and mediation

This chapter provides:

- an understanding of what parents can expect from the assessment and planning process;

- an outline of the responsibilities of the LA in providing and receiving relevant information;

- a summary of the role of parents in preparing for an EHC plan;

- a consideration of the implications of requesting a personal budget;

- a discussion of how to resolve disagreements;

- a discussion of CnYP in specific circumstances.

As we have already outlined, according to DfE (2019b) statistics, most CnYP should have their needs met through quality first teaching or universal provision. Less than 12 per cent of CnYP will have an identified SEN and will be in receipt of targeted or bespoke provision, as we have detailed in Part two. However, a small number of CnYP may require even greater support and an EHC plan may be requested. In this chapter we consider what CnYP and their parents can expect from this assessment and planning process and how any disagreement might be resolved.

What CnYP and parents can expect from the assessment and planning process

As we stated in Chapter 7, LAs **must** include the CnYP and their parents in ascertaining the nature of the CnYP's needs. The wishes of the individual concerned must be paramount in any decision-making and planning. This includes an understanding of the CnYP's strengths and capabilities as well as their aspirations. This approach, within the context of the family as well as other practitioners, is vital in bringing about effective provision for CnYP in their journey towards adulthood.

In considering an EHC plan, the assessment and planning process should be easy to understand and should avoid professional jargon. The CYPn and those who know them best should be enabled to articulate their interests, and the support should be tailored to meet the needs of the individual. This might mean the use of communication aids, an advocate, a translator or child-friendly formats. Necessary assessments should be undertaken in a way that minimises demands on families. Relevant practitioners should be brought together to be involved in agreeing an overall approach to this process. The role of liaising with and co-ordinating the contributions of such practitioners often falls to the SENCO. Additionally, the CoP (9.22) states that an '*outcomes focused and co-ordinated plan*' should be delivered through shared assessment and planning. In order to achieve such a plan, CnYP and their parents should be provided with appropriate information in formats they can access. There should be time for the CYPn and their parents to prepare for discussions and meetings, and there should be specific times within meetings where the views of the CYPn and their parents can be expressed (CoP, 9.24).

It is worth noting that while there has been a shift from the 2001 CoP, which saw parents as *informants*, the 2015 CoP still uses the language of *consultation* and *enablement* rather than empowerment and equality of partnership. Hodge and Runswick-Cole (2008, p 4) in their study of parent partnership suggested that such a position assumes that the '*decision making power lies elsewhere*' and while there may have been a move towards greater partnership with CnYP and their parents in the 2015 CoP, how far this has filtered through into practice is a question to be raised.

SCENARIO

Zamir is in Year 9. He has been receiving bespoke support through a personal learning mentor. Zamir is often absent from school, and when he does attend he is seen as disruptive. He does not see how attendance at school supports his interest in becoming a chef. Zamir is an EAL learner and speaks Punjabi at home as his grandmother who is his main carer does not speak English. She finds Zamir difficult to manage and there is social care involvement with the family. The school have decided that they want to pursue an EHC assessment and have planned a meeting where they intend to raise this. Those invited to the meeting are the school SENCO, learning mentor, Zamir's form tutor, attendance officer, school pastoral officer, EP, social worker and Zamir's grandmother.

CRITICAL QUESTIONS

Consider the scenario above and taking the perspective of Zainab or his grandmother, respond to these questions.

- What do you think this meeting is about?

- Who are all the people invited to this meeting? What is their contribution?

- Is there anyone at the meeting who you feel understands your position? Who is this and why?

- What preparation for this meeting would you like to have and why?

- How do you think your point of view is being represented?

- Is there someone you would have liked to be present at the meeting who is not invited? Who is this and why would you like them to be present?

- How do you think you might influence the decisions that will be made at this meeting?

- What outcomes would you look for from this meeting and why?

What CnYP and parents can expect from the LA

The onus for early discussions with CnYP and their parents on the EHC needs assessment lies with the LA. This also includes the option for personal budgets. The LA is obliged to work with CnYP and their parents to minimise the demands on family life and to provide them with advice and information so that their involvement in the assessment can be maximised. Meetings should be timed to be as convenient as possible to avoid disruption to family life, and other practitioners involved should be informed of meetings in sufficient time for them to attend.

Where possible, information should be made available to the CYPn and their family through a single point of personal contact. This key working approach should enable the CYPn to access holistic support through the effective co-ordination of health, social care and education or voluntary, private or independent sectors. Additionally, key working support should provide emotional and practical support for CnYP and their parents. This includes empowering them to make decisions, being an advocate, facilitating multi-agency meetings and supporting a joint assessment process (CoP, 2.21).

How CnYP and parents contribute to preparing for an EHC plan

Once it has been agreed that an EHC assessment should be requested, each step of the process should be carried out in a timely manner as we previously outlined in Chapter 7. Any disagreements and difficulties between parties should be resolved according to the statutory guidelines. While CnYP and their parents may wish to support the process to be carried out more swiftly, they should not at any stage feel under pressure to make decisions they are not ready for (CoP, 9.39).

As vital as it is to include CnYP and their parents in the decision to make a request for an EHC assessment, their information is but one part of the plethora of information that should be provided by other practitioners from health, education and social care. The LA must ensure that any representation or supporting evidence from CnYP and their parents is available to all those providing advice; this does beg the question as to the weight and value given to different practitioners' evidence alongside that of the evidence from the CYPn or their parents. According to research by Sales and Vincent (2018, p 71) 'what happens in practice will be influenced to a large extent by the actual professionals involved and their personal views on the value of parental input'.

Once all the evidence and information has been submitted to the LA, the decision as to whether an EHC plan is issued or not lies with LA officers, who need to weigh all the evidence provided. The CYPn's voice at this point can only be heard through the strength of their representation and evidence. Sales and Vincent's research (2018) showed that professionals thought that outcomes from the EHC process were not always based on need, but influenced by a number of factors such as whether the CYPn is considered to be *high profile* (ie is a looked-after child), how well a parent is able to advocate for a CYPn and how provision will be funded. Should an EHC plan not be issued following an assessment, then the CYPn and their parent have the right to appeal to SENDIST within a specific 16 week time frame (CoP, 9.57).

CRITICAL QUESTIONS

Consider the following questions from the perspective of your practice.

* What attitude do you have towards the evidence parents may provide as part of the request for an EHC plan? What influences this attitude?

* What are the differences in culture, processes and working practice between members of your professional practice and other practitioners? How might these be overcome?

The resolution of disagreement and mediation

Riddell et al (2009) outline how early resolution of disagreement should be pursued in order to avoid unnecessary anxiety, stress and financial commitment for all parties concerned. In addition to disagreement resolution, parents can choose to make use of mediation arrangements (CoP, 11.5). These are specifically related to decisions surrounding EHC needs assessments and plans. LAs **must** enable CnYP and their parents to receive information about mediation so that, if they wish, they can take part in this process before a possible appeal to the Tribunal (CoP, 11.14).

Those who act as mediators should be appropriately trained. They should provide factual and unbiased information to the CYPn and their parents. The mediation process should involve a meeting between the relevant parties at a place and time which is convenient to all. This information **must** be communicated to the CYPn and their parents at least five working days before the meeting is due to take place. It is the responsibility of the mediator to ensure the nature of the disagreement is clarified and that both sides are prepared for the mediation meeting. The CoP reiterates the importance of the views of the CYPn being obtained and represented (CoP, 11.38), therefore an advocate or adviser may be present.

It is important to note that an appeal to SENDIST cannot be registered unless mediation has been considered. However, despite the two processes of disagreement resolution and mediation being available to parents, the number of appeals to SENDIST has risen over the past few years. According to government figures (DfE, 2019c), there were 4108 appeals registered in 2014 compared with 6023 for the year 2018.

Truss (2008) describes how a parent became convinced something was wrong with her son. After several unproductive conversations with school staff, she decided to engage a private psychologist. When this did not seem to help, she turned back to the school. The SENCO promised to refer her son to other practitioners; however, this did not happen. Eventually a statutory assessment took place and the process of writing a statement (which is the predecessor of the EHC plan) began. The parent was advised to seek legal advice as to the content of the proposed statement and an appeal to SENDIST was lodged.

CRITICAL QUESTIONS

Referring to the summary from Truss (2008) above and taking the perspective of the parent or SENCO, consider:

*   how would you ensure that agreed actions have taken place?

*   how would you develop and maintain a productive working relationship?

Considering the expectations of the mediation process as we have outlined in this chapter and which is explained in more detail in Chapter 11 of the CoP:

*   how would you try to ensure that a tribunal would not be necessary?

The right to request a personal budget

Once an EHC plan is issued, parents or the YPn to whom the EHC plan applies has the right to request a personal budget. This is the amount of money identified by the LA to deliver the provision outlined in the EHC plan where the parent or YPn is involved in obtaining some or all provision (CoP, 9.101). Personal budgets should take into account a holistic perspective of the EHC plan (CoP, 9.99). Therefore, there is an expectation that services across education, health and social care should develop and agree a fair and equitable approach to the allocation of funding. This should result in each service contributing to the personal budget as identified by the CYPn's need. Information about services that lend themselves to the use of personal budgets **must** be made available as part of the LO.

As part of the PCP approach in developing the EHC plan, an indicative figure for the personal budget can be identified, which must be enough to cover the provision that is agreed in the EHC plan. Detailed records of terms under which payment for special educational provision is made should be kept and the agreement of these terms by parents or YP confirmed. The 2015 CoP makes it clear that while the YPn and/or their parent can claim responsibility for the way the personal budget is used, this can only be if certain conditions laid down by the LA are adhered to. For example, any person employed by the YPn or their parent and working within the CYPn's educational setting must conform to the policies and procedures of the institution (CoP, 9.104). Additionally, a consideration of a personal budget must involve a judgement as to whether this is an efficient use of the LA's resources (CoP, 9.106).

CnYP in specific circumstances

In this chapter we discuss the needs of CnYP educated out of area, CnYP with SEN who are in alternative provision and YP in youth custody. Ensuring the continuity of provision through an EHC plan poses particular difficulties for these CnYP as they will be either in education away from home, or in specialist provision.

CnYP educated out of area

Where a CYPn with SEN is being educated out of area, the LA where the CYPn usually lives should make the decision as to whether an assessment for an EHC plan is required. Where an EHC plan is already in place, the LA where the CYPn normally lives **must** make sure that the provision set out in the EHC plan is being made and that the EHC plan is reviewed annually. Where a CYPn is placed out of area by an LA, then they **must** pay appropriate costs, including if the placement is an independent special school, non-maintained special school or a residential placement. Residential placements must be secured as close as possible to the CYPn's home and after having regard for the views and wishes of the CYPn and their parents (CoP, 10.26–29).

CnYP with SEN in alternative provision

Where the LA arranges education for a CYPn other than at school, they are considered to be in alternative provision. This provision is for CnYP who find mainstream provision difficult and includes pupil referral units, alternative provision academies, alternative pro-vision free schools and online learning. The education **must** be full time unless the LA considers it is in the CYPn's best interests for a reduced level of education to be given. Alternative provision **must** consider the requirements specified in the CYPn's EHC plan. This plan should be reviewed regularly and adapted as necessary (CoP, 10.39–10.46). If a CYPn in alternative provision does not have an EHC plan, then their needs should be provided for within the graduated approach as we have detailed in Part two.

YP with SEN who are in youth custody

YP in youth custody are those who have been remanded or sentenced to youth accommo-dation in England. Youth accommodation might mean a Young Offender Institution, Secure Training Centre, Secure Children's Home or Secure College. YP in such accommodation are aged 18 and under and are referred to as a '*detained person*' (CoP, 10.60). LAs and youth offending teams (YOTs) as well as those who are responsible in youth accommodation **must** have regard to and adhere to the principles set out in the CoP as a whole (CoP, 10.64). On entering custody, the YPn is expected to undergo an assessment of literacy and numeracy and, if necessary, screening to consider whether SEN may be identified. Such assessments should provide the basis on which individual provision is offered and high quality support provided regardless of whether an EHC plan is in place. This should be put in place as soon as possible to ensure the needs of the YPn are met. If a detained person does not have an EHC plan, an assessment can be requested (CoP, 10.68). The process of identification and the support for such YP follows the same process as for any other individual as we have already outlined.

As with any YPn, the wishes, views and feelings of a YPn in youth custody **must** be considered when making decisions concerning their individual support. Parents, including those who have parental responsibility or who provide care for the YPn, should also be included in these decision-making processes. The CoP states that appropriate information, advice and support **must** be provided in order for them to be involved (CoP, 10.65). Additionally, there should be a clear understanding of any SEN and high quality support provided. Such understanding relies on good collaboration between education, health and social care services and should plan for continuity of provision when the YPn enters custody and when they leave it (CoP, 10.65).

It is a statutory requirement for LAs to maintain an existing EHC plan while the YPn is in custody, and to review it when they are released (CoP, 10.74). Where the EHC plan specifies health care provision, this **must** be arranged while the detained person is in youth accommodation. This is the same for any social care needs, for example maintaining continued contact with the social worker. If SEN, health or social care provision detailed in the EHC plan cannot be arranged, then provision that is as close as possible to that specified **must** be organised (CoP, 10.67).

SCENARIO

Sarah is 17 years old. She has been given a 2 year custodial sentence, which she is serving in a Young Offenders, Institute, away from her home county. She is having difficulties accessing the curriculum, especially recording her work in a timely manner. The person in charge of the Institute has asked the LA to carry out an assessment of her needs. There is some urgency given her sentence comes to an end in 3 months' time.

IMPLICATIONS FOR PRACTICE

Adopting the role of a social worker and using the relevant sections of Chapter 10 of the CoP (10.66–10.70 and 10.81–10.83), answer the following questions.

*   What are the timelines for assessment for Sarah?

*   What sources of information might you be asked to provide as part of the assessment process?

*   Who might you liaise with?

Conclusion

CnYP whose needs are considered to be significant are entitled to provision that meets their needs and prepares them for adulthood. For some CnYP this means provision through an EHC plan. The involvement of CnYP and their parents in the assessment and planning of this additional provision is vital. All practitioners must work together to ensure the wishes, views and feelings of all CnYP, no matter what their circumstances, are considered and that the provision made reflects these desires.

Further reading and web-based materials

This research investigates the experiences of parents in Hull since the introduction of the 2014 SEND legislation. It identified what was working well and what could be improved.

Holland, J and Pell, G (2017) Parental Perceptions of the 2014 SEND Legislation. *Pastoral Care in Education*, 35(4): 293–311.

This website provides a region-by-region advice and support service for parents, contact details of SENDIASS for each LA and how to access independent advice and support area by area.

councilfordisabledchildren.org.uk/information-advice-and-support-services-network (accessed 9 August 2019).

9 The education practitioner's responsibility

Who do we mean by education practitioner?

What is the role of the education practitioner?

The education practitioner's responsibility

Transition

What is the education practitioner's responsibility?

Preparing for adulthood

Working with other practitioners

This chapter provides:

- an understanding of what is meant by education practitioner;

- an outline of the role of the education practitioner including the expectation of working with other practitioners;

- a discussion of transition and preparation for adulthood.

Who do we mean by education practitioner?

While education practitioners feature significantly in guidance documents regarding CnYP with SEN, HPs and SCPs feature less strongly. The SEND CoP 2015 is written with a heavy education focus, which may be understandable as CnYP up to the age of 19 years should be in some kind of educational provision. However, in practice, this emphasis on education within guidance can lead to the SENCOs and teachers feeling that they carry the main responsibility for supporting CnYP with SEN, even when the appropriate provision for a CYPn requires expertise and professional skill beyond that of their own.

Education practitioners are generally considered to be teachers including SENCOs and headteachers. However, depending on the age of the CYPn or the setting they attend, there are a number of other education practitioners who may be involved. Some of these are:

- the child's key worker – a specific named worker whose role is to build positive relationships with the CYPn and act as an advocate as necessary;

- the Portage worker (for children 0–2 years) – working with families and their children to help them develop a good quality of life and experience;

- childminder (usually preschool) – providing childcare usually during school or parents' working hours;

- support staff, eg TAs, learning mentors – often working one to one with CnYP, with small groups, supporting whole-class work or providing personal care;

- EP – a psychologist who supports CnYP to develop and learn more effectively and also carries out tests which may indicate a specific learning difficulty such as dyslexia;

- specialist teachers – these include teachers of the deaf or visually impaired and teachers of children with autism.

Some of these practitioners are based in one particular school or multi-academy trust (MAT), whereas others, such as the EP or specialist teacher, may be part of the LA traded service or employed privately by the educational setting.

What is the role of the education practitioner?

Between the ages of 2 and 3 years, children in England should be assessed using the EYFS framework. This assessment should be completed by '*a practitioner who knows the child well and who works with them within the setting*' (National Children's Bureau, 2012). This is most often an education practitioner. The monitoring and assessment of a CYPn's learning and development should be an integral part of their educational experience until transition to adulthood and potentially into employment.

The 2015 CoP states that all CnYP are entitled to an education that is appropriate to their needs, has high standards and enables them to fulfil their potential. CnYP should be enabled to:

- *achieve their best*

- *become confident individuals living fulfilling lives, and*

- *make a successful transition into adulthood, whether into employment, further or higher education or training.*

(CoP, 6.1)

Chapters 4–6 of this book explain the process of assessment, identification and provision for CnYP with SEN through the assess, plan, do, review cycle, known as the graduated approach. It is the responsibility of education practitioners at each age phase to ensure that all CnYP are supported and that the provision for them addresses their needs. This is the case whether the CYPn is in early years, primary, secondary or post-16 provision and whether they are receiving support through quality first teaching, through interventions, through targeted support or through an EHC plan.

What is the education practitioner's responsibility?

The education practitioner should do all they can to make suitable provision for the CYPn. Where this CYPn is making less than expected progress despite the support being offered within the setting, then the education practitioner should consider involving other specialists. These might include speech and language therapists, CAMHS, specialist teachers or EPs. Commissioning services should ensure that there are sufficient services to meet the needs of CnYP in that area and the LO should make it clear what support is available. Where CnYP's needs cannot be met despite relevant and purposeful action, then an EHC assessment should be considered (CoP, 6.63).

Working with other practitioners

Some children entering early years education may already have an identified disability, medical need or SEN. If this is the case, then careful liaison between other practitioners involved with the child is necessary in order to provide effective support. In practice the education practitioner is often the person who co-ordinates the support of the CYPn with SEN. However, they cannot make effective provision for such CnYP without the knowledge and expertise of other practitioners such as from health and social care. Therefore, it is vital for all practitioners who know the CYPn to play a full part in making provision for them.

Hall and Elliman (2003) identify a range of features that support effective working with practitioners across a range of services especially health and social care. Some of these are:

- *continuity of staffing within the team;*
- *effective communication;*
- *protected time for team meetings;*
- *clear delineation of tasks and objectives, individual responsibility, leadership and accountability;*
- *written team guidelines;*
- *good and shared record keeping;*
- *knowledge and respect for expertise of other team members;*
- *personal respect;*
- *ability to reach and keep to joint decisions.*

(Hall and Elliman, 2003, p 17)

CRITICAL QUESTIONS

From the perspective of your own role as a practitioner and using the features identified by Hall and Elliman (2003) consider the following.

- What elements of effective working across services have you experienced?
- Which features do you think are most often lacking and why?
- What can you do to develop effective working with other practitioners?

Similarly, Wenger outlines the importance of shared responsibility within a '*community of practice*' (1999, p 45). In order to bring about coherence of a community of practice of different and possibly diverse members, Wenger identifies three characteristics.

1. Mutual engagement – all participants doing whatever they are there to do.
2. Negotiation of a joint enterprise – all parties finding a way of working together, through discussion and despite differences and dilemmas, in order to achieve understood goals and outcomes.
3. Shared repertoire – includes shared routines, language, gestures and actions taken on board by all the members of the community of practice and which give meaning to the group and its members.

While Wenger acknowledges that communities of practice are not *'intrinsically beneficial or harmful'*, he also maintains that *'such communities hold the key to real transformation – the kind that has real effects on people's lives'* (Wenger, 1999, p 85). For CnYP with SEN to be supported holistically within a community of practice, it is therefore vital for all practitioners, whether from education, health or social care, to use their own unique expertise to work together for agreed outcomes. In doing so they should develop a shared way of working that embraces all members of the community including parents as well as the CYPn.

IMPLICATIONS FOR PRACTICE

- Consider to what extent your working relationships with other practitioners demonstrate (a) mutual engagement, (b) negotiation of a joint enterprise, (c) shared repertoire.

- From the perspective of an education practitioner, how can you ensure good provision for the individual needs of CnYP with SEN within an education culture of testing, raising standards and a narrow curriculum?

Transition

Transition into employment can often be a difficult journey for the YPn and their parents to navigate. Davies and Beamish (2009) recognise that in taking up employment, YP need support from committed and consistent adults such as teachers, family members and multi-agency teams. Above all this must involve high levels of partnership.

YP with SEN, regardless of whether they have an EHC plan or not, should be prepared by schools and colleges for adulthood and for life beyond education. This includes a review of their SEN provision or EHC plan and should enable the YPn and their family to engage with adult health and social care services. Chapter 8 of the CoP 2015 makes it clear that this vital transition should provide the YPn with clear timescales and information about what will happen when their EHC plan ends. While the YPn is in education or training, it is the responsibility of the LA to continue to maintain the EHC plan. Where a YPn aged between 19 and 25 has an EHC plan and attends an FE college, the YPn **must not** be charged tuition fees. However, FE colleges can charge a fee for YP who have SEN but do not have an EHC plan. Students who meet eligibility criteria can access funding through the Skills Funding Agency, now known as the Education and Skills Funding Agency. Where a YPn takes up an apprenticeship, they are fully funded for these employment opportunities.

Preparing for adulthood

YP in post-16 education or training, including school sixth forms, general FE colleges, specialist colleges and 16–19 academies, should be supported to participate in discussions about their aspirations and needs, and what support is required as they prepare for adulthood. Education practitioners within colleges should ensure that such support is provided and that this is based on reliable evidence. This support could include:

- *assistive technology;*
- *personal care provision;*
- *specialist tuition;*
- *note takers;*
- *interpreters;*
- *one-to-one, small group learning support;*
- *habilitation/independent living training;*
- *accessible information such as symbol-based materials;*
- *access to therapies.*

(CoP, 7.17)

It is the responsibility of LAs, schools and colleges to be aware of the different options available for disabled YP, and LAs should provide details of supported employment services within the LO. Education practitioners in colleges and post-16 provision should help YP to develop the skills valued by employers and provide them with first-hand experiences of work where possible. This might be through apprenticeships, traineeships or supported internships, all of which are available to YP with EHC plans. Such work placements should be carefully selected and supported in order to provide a positive work experience for the YPn.

The CoP (7.38) identifies that planning for adulthood means:

- *preparing for higher education and/or employment;*
- *independent living;*
- *participating in society;*
- *being healthy in adult life.*

These outcomes are intended to support the CYPn in having choice, including employment options, supportive relationships and friends. They should be a feature of discussion and forward planning, especially from the age of 14 years onwards.

IMPLICATIONS FOR PRACTICE

The Preparing for Adulthood (PfA) website explores these four key outcomes in relation to transition planning and supporting the CYPn's aspirations. Using the following link www. preparingforadulthood.org.uk/downloads/pfa-self-evaluation-tool and from the position of your practice, eg parent, education, health, social care, select the appropriate self-evaluation tool. Use this to respond to the following questions.

→

- What resources would you use to support a CYPn moving into adulthood?
- What practice would you employ to support effective transition?
- How would you ensure the four PfA outcomes are addressed?
- How would you ensure that relevant information is passed from one setting to another?
- Why might this be important and who should agree any transition plan?

Conclusion

This chapter has considered a range of different education practitioners and their role in working with CnYP with SEN. It outlines how such practitioners should ensure their own working practices are fully supportive of such CnYP throughout their educational journey, at all transition points, including into adulthood. Furthermore, it emphasises the importance of good communication with practitioners from other services. The role of HPs and SCPs in supporting CnYP with SEN is discussed in Chapters 10 and 11.

Further reading and web-based materials

This book provides up-to-date information about the practice of the SENCO. It is written as a handbook for practising SENCOs, but it is also useful for the senior leadership of a school as well as teachers and parents in understanding the strategic and practical role of the SENCO.

Cowne, E, Frankl, C and Gerschel, L (2019) *The SENCo Handbook: Leading and Managing a Whole School Approach*, 7th edition. London: Routledge.

In this research Alison Wren interviews TAs and pupils to ascertain their perspectives on the role that TAs play. Her research shows that there is a discrepancy in perception of what the TA role involves and recommends that there should be a clarification of role and expectation for both parties.

Wren, A (2017) Understanding the Role of the Teaching Assistant: Comparing the Views of Pupils with SEN and TAs Within Mainstream Primary Schools. *Support for Learning*, 32(1): 4–19.

The National Portage Association website provides information about the Portage service and how it can support preschool children with SEN and their families. Portage is a home-visit-based service. You can also find details of the Portage service for your area on the LO.

What Is Portage?: www.portage.org.uk/about/what-portage (accessed 14 January 2020).

10   The health practitioner's responsibility

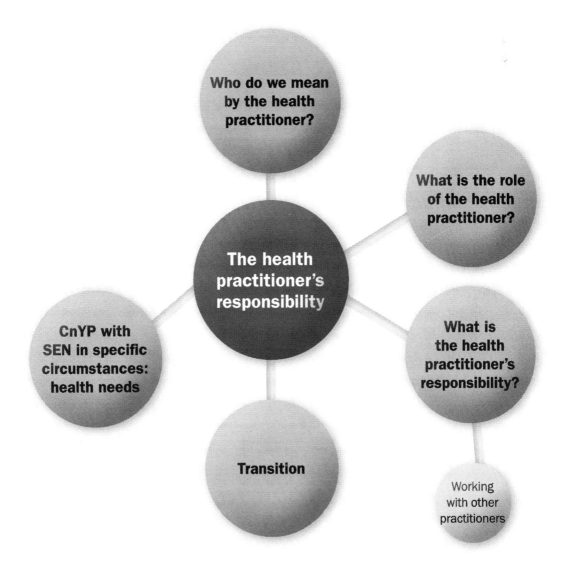

Who do we mean by the health practitioner?

What is the role of the health practitioner?

The health practitioner's responsibility

CnYP with SEN in specific circumstances: health needs

What is the health practitioner's responsibility?

Transition

Working with other practitioners

This chapter provides:

- an understanding of what is meant by the health practitioner (HP);
- an outline of the role of the HP;
- an understanding of CnYP in alternative provision, with health care needs.

Who do we mean by health practitioners?

A CYPn with SEN is likely to have contact with HPs. At the start of a CYPn's life, this will often be the midwife closely followed by a health visitor. More recently, there has been a reduction in the numbers of health visitors (Bunn, 2019) which may mean that visits are less frequent. Throughout a CYPn's life it is the general practitioner (GP) who is the main point of access to appropriate medical and health provision. Other HPs who may provide medical and health care include the following.

- Health visitor: a qualified nurse or midwife working in the community to promote good health and prevent illness by offering practical help and advice. Health visitors usually provide support to children aged 0–5 years.
- School nurse: working in a school setting to provide support through assessment and intervention. School nurses usually provide support to CnYP from aged 5 years till transition to adult services.
- SALT: supporting CnYP who may have speech, language and communication problems, or difficulties in swallowing, drinking or eating.
- OT: providing practical support for carrying out day-to-day activities.
- Physiotherapist: providing practical support with regard to problems with movement and mobility.
- Paediatrician: may be hospital based providing medical care, or community based with responsibility for CnYP who may have developmental, social or behavioural needs.
- Psychiatrist: specialist doctor in mental health related needs.
- CAMHS practitioner: this can include psychiatrists, psychologists, social workers, nurses, support workers, OTs, psychological therapists.
- Surgeon, eg orthopaedic; ear, nose and throat; cardiology.
- Other allied HPs, eg dietician, art therapist, podiatrist.

What is the role of the health practitioner?

Valuing People (DH, 2001) introduced health action plans (HAPs) for people with learning disabilities. These plans should take account of the need for health interventions in order to remain healthy. The responsibility for their development should rest with GPs and primary care nurses. These plans do not, unlike an EHC plan, have a standard format. It is unclear how these two documents fit together, but a HAP may help to inform assessment for an EHC plan.

The role of the HP may vary depending on the age of the CYPn, but in essence they must provide information and advice as part of an initial request for an EHC plan assessment. This should be detailed, specific and quantified and take account of the aspirations and planned outcomes. If an EHC plan is in place, then as part of an annual review process, the HP **must** co-operate and provide up-to-date information. This should include details of provision, progress to date and recommendations for future provision (CoP, 9.169).

Children may have paediatric involvement from an early age. Ko (2015) suggests that paediatricians should provide high quality medical advice, which is important in order to inform the content of an EHC plan. The CoP advocates that this is the role of all HPs, not just a paediatrician. The British Association for Community Child Health (BACCH) together with the British Academy of Childhood Disability (BACD) (2014) provide paediatricians with recommendations when providing evidence for the development of an EHC plan. These include:

• acknowledging concerns of the CYPn, their family and other practitioners;

• detailed medical development, family and functional history;

• a systematic physical examination;

• observational assessment;

• investigations and onwards referral.

CRITICAL QUESTIONS

Taking the role of a community paediatrician and from your own knowledge and understanding, using the list above consider the following.

• If you were involved in the support and care of a CYPn with SEN how you would follow these recommendations? What implications might they have for you?

• When writing your advice, how would you ensure the language you use is accessible and meaningful to those who implement the EHC plan?

• What kind of information might you include to help ensure positive outcomes for the CYPn?

Other HPs are likely to become involved as more is known about the needs of the CYPn, especially if there has been a request for assessment for an EHC plan.

What is the health practitioner's responsibility?

The Children and Families Act 2014 makes it clear that health bodies such as CCGs, NHS trusts or NHS foundation trusts have a mandatory responsibility for children under compulsory school age where they are of the opinion that a child has or may have SEN or a disability. This requires them to inform the parent of this opinion and to provide an opportunity for this to be discussed (Section 23).

Parts I and II of this book identify the importance of collaborative working between all practitioners. The guide to the CoP for HPs also recognises the need for this: '*for too long health has been the missing partner in the SEND system*' (DfE and DH, 2016, p 4). This was reinforced further in the 2019 Education Committee SEND report which very clearly identifies that '*unless health and social care are at the table we are no further on*' (House of Commons, 2019a, p 4).

Broach et al (2015) identify that health services are critically important for many CnYP with SEN and/or disability and, where health provision is included in an EHC plan, this has to be arranged by the NHS. HPs should be cognisant of the NHS constitution (National Health Service Act, 2006; Health Act, 2009) especially the four statements of right, namely to:

- access NHS services without being refused access on unreasonable grounds;
- receive treatment and care that not only meets need, but reflects personal preference;
- expect services to meet need to be put in place;
- not be unlawfully discriminated against.

IMPLICATIONS FOR PRACTICE

An OT working with a family of a 5-year-old child has identified that the child has signifi-cant sensory processing difficulties. The EHC plan identifies that the child needs weekly one-to-one sessions of sensory processing therapy. The OT has a full case load and there is no other OT who can undertake that type of specialist work. From your own practitioner perspective, consider the following.

- If the lack of therapist constituted unreasonable grounds, how would you try and resolve the issue?

- How would you determine whether this was unlawful discrimination?

It is important to note the strategic importance of health when supporting CnYP with an EHC plan that includes health provision. There is a right for this to be provided by the NHS. For health services, this means a specific post of Designated Medical Officer (DMO) or Designated Clinical Officer (DCO) has to be in place (CoP, 3.45). In some areas these roles are interchangeable and are usually fulfilled by a paediatrician, but could also be a '*suitably competent, qualified and experienced nurse or other health professional*' (CoP, 3.48). They have a defined role in supporting local arrangements and provide the point of contact for LAs, schools and colleges when seeking health advice on a CYPn (CoP, 3.46). They also have an oversight across all HPs, liaising and gathering information for the EHC plan, having oversight of the plan once it is in place and being involved in the joint area inspections.

As with any person involved in supporting CnYP with SEN, it is the HP's responsibility to work with other practitioners in order to secure positive outcomes. It is important that health and education systems work closely together (NHS England, 2018a). However, there is no explicit statutory obligation for the NHS or the LA to act as the lead agency in securing provision. Broach et al (2015, 5.25) identified that where services are not co-ordinated there may be '*drift*' and services may blame each other for the failing. In practice, it is more than likely that the SENCO will take the lead, hence placing more emphasis on education and less on health and social care.

A key aspect of this responsibility is to ensure effective working practices and communication between all parties. Chapter 9 of this book discusses how '*communities of practice*' (Wenger, 1999, p 45) help ensure effective partnership working. It is important that HPs help to establish protocols for communication and sharing of information. The Lenehan review (2017) recognised the need for effective communication and that families should have one professional point of contact. This could be the HP.

Working with other practitioners

Sales and Vincent (2018) identified where multi-agency working was good, parents were much more satisfied with the EHC plan process and subsequent support, although they noted that the HPs' attendance at review meetings was not common. Boesley and Crane (2018) also identify the need for collaboration between services in order for individuals to be supported effectively. However, in practice this is not always straightforward. Popular perception considers that there is a hierarchy of status between teachers and doctors. Doctors are considered to have specialist knowledge, defined by Jackson (1970, p 7) as creating a '*distinct mystique*'. For teachers, the rise of mass education has resulted in weakening the '*distinct mystique*' as the tasks they perform are '*within the general competence of those who have been taught themselves*' (Jackson, 1970, p 14). Within the partnerships, the voice of the medical practitioner may be dominant or more attention may be given to their recommendations.

Transition

CnYP will undergo a number of transitions through their journey to adulthood. HPs should be involved at all transition points by providing up-to-date assessment and information to help inform the next stage of the CYPn's journey. A key transition point is to adult health services. This usually occurs at the age of 18. For CnYP, especially those with complex health needs, it is important that there is a continuity of provision to adult services (CoP,

8.54). Under the age of 18, a CYPn can be under the care of a single paediatrician, but in adult services they are much more likely to have several consultants, especially if co-occurrence of SEN exists.

CnYP with SEN in specific circumstances: health needs

Some CnYP with SEN may have clearly identified health needs. These may require education in alternative provision with additional consideration to ensure appropriate support and resources are in place. This alternative provision must be on a par with that of mainstream provision and it is the LA's responsibility to ensure this is in place. This type of provision can include hospital school, home education or specialist provision attached to mainstream schools such as hearing impairment units. The role and responsibility of the HP for CnYP with health needs does not differ from that of the HP for any CYPn. They must provide good quality support and provision to prevent the CYPn slipping behind their peers in terms of progress. Chapter 10 of the CoP provides more information for practitioners to refer to in order to ensure effective provision.

IMPLICATIONS FOR PRACTICE

Aleem is 10 years old. He has cerebral palsy and, as a result, a range of complex health needs. In his Year 5 annual review of his EHC plan, his parents express concerns that when he moves on to his local secondary school, he will not get the appropriate support that he needs. Taking the role of the HP, eg physiotherapist or SALT, you have been asked to provide information as part of the annual review.

Consider the following.

- Referring to CoP 9.167, identify the provision that might be required to ensure good progress and outcomes for Aleem, including a positive transition into secondary school.

- Who would you collect relevant information from?

- What might the challenges be of collecting information?

- At what point in the process might you need to involve the CCG? Would this be the responsibility of the HP?

Conclusion

In this chapter we have examined the role of the HP and in particular the part they play in supporting CnYP to access learning. For some CnYP this may mean provision other than in a mainstream setting. The importance of working as part of a 'community of practice' is never more apparent than when trying to support CnYP with health care needs, some of which may be very complex.

Further reading and web-based materials

Advice for CCGs, HPs and LAs. This document looks at the SEND CoP specifically from the point of view of health and outlines implications for practice.

DfE and DH (2016) *0 to 25 SEND Code of Practice: A Guide for Health Practitioners.* [online] Available at: assets.publishing.service.gov.uk/government/uploads/system/ uploads/attachment_data/file/502913/Health_Professional_Guide_to_the_Send_ Code_of_Practice.pdf (accessed 6 July 2019).

Guidance that LAs **must** adhere to when providing support for CnYP who cannot attend a school placement because of complex health care needs.

DfE (2013) *Ensuring a Good Education for Children Who Cannot Attend School Because of Health Needs: Statutory Guidance.* [online] Available at: assets.publishing.service.gov. uk/government/uploads/system/uploads/attachment_data/file/269469/health_ needs_guidance__-_revised_may_2013_final.pdf (accessed 14 July 2019).

This video helps the viewer to gain a better understanding of the role of DMO/DCO using real-life case studies.

Designated Medical Officers/Designated Clinical Officer for SEND role (2019). [online] Available at: www.youtube.com/watch?v=Mg7YCNqcyGg&feature=youtu.be (accessed 14 July 2019).

Statutory guidance for governing bodies of maintained schools and proprietors of academies in England.

DfE (2015) *Supporting Pupils at School with Medical Conditions.* [online] Available at: assets.publishing.service.gov.uk/government/uploads/system/uploads/attachment_ data/file/803956/supporting-pupils-at-school-with-medical-conditions.pdf (accessed 10 August 2019).

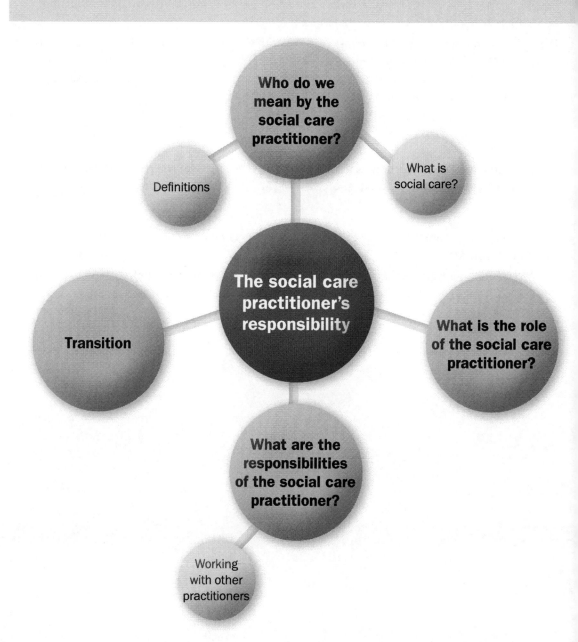

> This chapter provides:
>
> - an understanding of what is meant by the SCP and what social care entails in the context of CnYP with SEND;
>
> - an outline of the role of the SCP including the expectation of working with other practitioners;
>
> - a discussion of transition including preparation for adulthood.

For many CnYP their social care need is provided for by family, friends and support/voluntary groups. However, there may be occasions when a particular type of support is needed, and this can best be provided by social care services.

Who do we mean by the social care practitioner?

Unlike HPs, where there are a large number of defined roles, as identified in Chapter 10 of the CoP, with SCPs this is not the case. SCPs include qualified social workers with particular areas of expertise and social care workers who may have different job titles, eg care assistant, support worker, but who in essence provide daily care and support for CnYP. This support can be of a personal nature or by providing help towards independence, eg travel training, attendance at social activities.

Definitions

It is important to note that legal definitions for CnYP with SEN and disability differ in legislation. The Children Act (1989, section 17(11)) provides the following definition of a disabled child, albeit in language that we consider to be outdated and driven by a medical model perspective:

> *a child is disabled if he is blind, deaf or dumb or suffers from mental disorder of any kind or is substantially and permanently handicapped by illness, injury or congenital deformity or such other disability as may be prescribed.*

If a CYPn is defined as disabled under the Act, then they are automatically a '*child in need*' under the same Act section 17(10)(c). Once this has been determined, there is a duty on the LA's social care teams to provide appropriate assessment and social care services where deemed necessary. This should be recorded in section H of the EHC plan. These services will include providing social care advice to all education providers, contributing to reviews and ensuring, in particular, that a needs assessment of a YPn who has reached the age of 18 is properly co-ordinated. This assessment identifies eligibility for adult social care services. Where a CYPn has received social care under the age of 18 and this is deemed a continuing need, the LA must not stop provision until adult services have assessed this and necessary provision has been put in place.

What is social care?

While we have attempted to provide a definition of social care in the context of SEN and disability, despite an extensive search a clear definition is elusive. However, the provision of social care needs to take account of the principles underpinning the CoP (DfE and DH, 2015, p 6). SCPs are required to work within the same statutory framework as education and HPs, yet DfE (2014b) advice for SCPs has no statutory basis, once again placing the onus upon education.

The CoP separates social care provision into two elements. These comprise care needs as a result of disability and as identified under the CSDPA 1970 and other social care needs not provided for under this Act, which include early help, children in need and safeguarding assessments.

What is the role of the social care practitioner?

When additional practical help and support is needed over and above what a family can offer, this should be provided by social services through the LA. This can include help both inside the home and in the community and is detailed in the CSDPA (1970) section 2(4). According to this statutory document it includes provision such as:

- personal care, eg help to wash and dress, getting in and out of bed;
- recreational facilities in the home, eg TV, radio, computer;
- recreational facilities outside the home, eg outings, games;
- assistance to take advantage of education;
- travel, eg help to and from home to an activity or day centre;
- adaptations to the home, eg handrails, wet rooms;
- holidays and short breaks;
- meals at home or elsewhere;
- telephone and other related equipment.

SCENARIO

We met Jayden in Chapter 4 of this book. He is 17. His aspiration is to be a motor mechanic. He has been diagnosed as having dyslexia and ADHD. He finds concentration difficult and does not always take his medication. He does not always make good friendship choices and is often tired. His grandmother takes him to college every day by car, but both the college and his house are on a bus route.

IMPLICATIONS FOR PRACTICE

Adopting the role of the SCP and referring to types of provision listed above, consider the following.

*   How you would assess what support Jayden might need as he moves into adulthood?

*   What other practitioners might you need to liaise with?

*   What would a package of support contain?

*   Who would provide the support?

What are the responsibilities of the social care practitioner?

The SCP's responsibility is to respond to a request for social care assessment and to carry out that assessment within 45 days, as part of their duty under the Children Act 1989. As a result of the assessment, any provision that has been identified will need to be put into place. In practice, requests for this provision will usually have to go before a local resource panel who make the final decision. In our experience this decision is often driven by financial constraints. As part of the social care needs assessment the SCP should ensure they ask questions of both the CYPn and their parents. This should seek to elicit information to ensure that the CYPn is safe and that will enable the SCP to have a greater understanding of need. This is in order to provide appropriate social care support. These could include the following questions.

*   What is important to the CYPn?

*   What is going well in their lives and what could be improved?

*   What hobbies and interests do they have? Would they like to develop them or new ones?

*   What support do they receive from family and friends?

*   What challenges do they face?

When carrying out an assessment, the SCP should be focused on outcomes, as outlined in the Children and Families Act 2014. This can be best understood by using the CDC's pyramid as discussed in Chapter 2 and should link directly to the CYPn's aspirations.

The social care needs assessment can lead to a number of outcomes. If there should be continuing involvement from social care, then the SCP should develop a social care plan and agree a plan of action with other practitioners. It may be that an EHC plan is also deemed necessary and if this is the case the social care aspect must be included in part H of the plan.

The SCP is also responsible for ensuring that they signpost CnYP and their parents to what is available under the LO. The LA **must** seek social care advice as part of the EHC plan assessment (CoP, 9.46) and should include details if appropriate of any child in need or child protection assessments (CoP, 9.49).

The LA's social care team have a number of responsibilities. They:

- **must** secure social care provision;

- **must** undertake reviews of any CYPn with an EHC plan;

- should provide education providers, such as nurseries, schools and colleges, with social care advice;

- should ensure effective co-ordination across health, education and social care to make sure that looked-after CnYP and care leavers have a clear pathway, avoiding duplication.

(CoP, 3.49)

CRITICAL QUESTION

- Referring to the **must** and should statements set out above, what are the challenges for the SCP when trying to fulfil their duties as part of a multi-agency team?

Social care is not only relevant to CnYP themselves, but also to their parents. The pressure of supporting CnYP with SEND can have an impact on parental self-esteem and well-being and contribute to financial difficulties. As a result, LAs should consider what support parents might need (CoP, 3.57). Information about the statutory and non-statutory role of social care (known as early help) is available on the LO.

Working with other practitioners

As we have already discussed in previous chapters, collaboration between education, health and social care services can be problematic. The LA must ensure that all practitioners work effectively together, particularly in relation to transition (CoP, 4.17). The dilemma for practitioners is how to achieve this. Frank (2005) discusses the importance of recognising difference in others, or 'seeing the face' (p 116) of the other. He uses the word 'alterity' (p 115) to describe this respect. In essence this is about recognising the differences between people (different practitioners, parents, CnYP) and working towards shared meaning – towards blended practice.

CRITICAL QUESTIONS

- From the perspective of your own role as a practitioner and using the concept Frank (2005) identifies, what skills might you need to ensure you are *seeing the face* of other practitioners who will be working with CnYP with SEND?

- How might you encourage collaborative working, especially at the key transition from child to adult services?

Transition

If the CYPn has an EHC plan the LA should ensure that transition is well planned and is discussed as part of the annual review. If there is no EHC plan but care needs have been identified, a statutory social care plan must be in place.

Transition into employment is a key component for some YP entering adulthood. A good programme is essential if aspirations towards employment are to be realised. Hanson et al (2017) identified five key areas to enable an effective transition to take place.

1. Providing and maintaining support from an early point in secondary education until employment is secured.

2. Accessing support and relevant development opportunities, eg careers guidance, specific skills training.

3. Involving families.

4. Providing hands-on experience of working with employers and other people, eg supported internships.

5. Ensuring support is available in the workplace.

The CoP sets out further details with regard to pathways to employment (CoP, 8.31–8.38).

Conclusion

In this chapter we have examined the role of the SCP and a recurring theme of good communication and partnership working. Interestingly the government places emphasis on this at a strategic level and as a result has combined the separate departments for health and social care into one DHSC.

Further reading and web-based materials

A very useful briefing providing help for all those who have responsibility for co-ordinating the information as part of the EHC plan assessment process.

CDC (2016) *Identifying the Social Care Needs of Disabled Children and Young People and Those With SEN As Part of Education Health and Care Needs Assessments.* [online]

Available at: councilfordisabledchildren.org.uk/sites/default/files/field/attachemnt/ Identifying%20the%20social%20care%20needs_0.pdf (accessed 12 July 2019).

This document provides practical information for all practitioners on developing and implementing supported internships.

DfE (2014) *Supported Internships: Advice for FE Colleges, Sixth Forms in Academies, Maintained and Non-Maintained Schools, Independent Specialist Providers, Other Providers of Study Programmes and Local Authorities.* [online] Available at: baseuk.org/ sites/default/files/knowledge/Supported%20Internships%20guidance/supported_ internships_guidance.pdf (accessed 22 July 2019).

An organisation that supports families with guidance and information. This section gives clear details of the transition process from child to adult services, together with links to supporting documents.

Available at: contact.org.uk/advice-and-support/social-care/moving-into-adult-services/ (accessed 22 July 2019).

A helpful website for CnYP, their parents and practitioners, with resources grouped under themed areas.

Available at: send.excellencegateway.org.uk/employers-and-employability (accessed 16 September 2019).

A comprehensive website that provides information about early help and support for CnYP at any stage in their life in order to improve outcomes. While the primary focus is upon CnYP, support is also provided to their families.

NSPCC Learning: Early help (or early intervention). Available at: learning.nspcc. org.uk/safeguarding-child-protection/early-help-early-intervention (accessed 10 August 2019).

12 Implementing the education, health and care plan

This chapter provides:

- an understanding of how an EHC plan is implemented;
- an understanding of the expectations for education, health and social care;
- an outline of alternative arrangements for provision;
- a discussion of research findings regarding implementation of EHC plans;
- details of local area SEND inspections.

The implementation process

An EHC plan is the document that describes the SEN of a CYPn, the agreed outcomes to be achieved and the support required to achieve those outcomes. This stated provision **must** be provided by the CYPn's LA. The final EHC plan is signed and dated by the LA officer with delegated responsibility (CoP, 9.125) and at this point it becomes active.

Implementation before or after compulsory school age

For children under the age of 2, an EHC plan may be issued to enable access to a particular specialist service, such as Portage, or peripatetic services for hearing or visual impairment that otherwise could not be accessed (CoP, 9.145). For children aged 2–5, an EHC plan may stipulate additional support or placement at a particular education setting best suited to meet their particular needs. For children who are close to 5 years of age, an EHC plan may be deemed necessary in order for the receiving setting to plan and prepare a smooth transition into statutory education.

Implementation of an EHC plan for YP aged 19 to 25 ensures that there is a longer period of time for them to achieve the identified outcomes within their education, training and preparation for adulthood (CoP, 9.151). There is no automatic entitlement for an EHC plan to be maintained to age 25, but, where the EHC plan is not maintained, the LA must be satisfied that the outcomes have been achieved.

What parents and CnYP can expect

For many CnYP, the receipt of the final EHC plan will entail little immediate change within their existing mainstream setting, but for others it will necessitate change, eg of educational placement. The DfE (2019d) SEN statistics evidenced 69 per cent of new EHC plans (issued in 2018) being made for mainstream settings while those CnYP aged 5 to 16 with existing plans are split evenly between mainstream and special schools. However, sometimes expectations about what the EHC plan is designed to achieve do not match up in reality and there can be a perceived mismatch. For example, in practice we have been aware a parent might expect the allocated funding to provide full-time, one-to-one TA support for their CYPn, but the education setting may use some of the funding to purchase resources that they believe will support the delivery of identified outcomes.

Sections F (educational provision), G (health provision), H1 and H2 (social care provision) of the EHC plan set out in detail what the CYPn is legally entitled to receive to progress towards preparation for adulthood. The provision is required to be implemented exactly as stated, with the intention that the help and support should improve the CYPn's experience of education (CoP, 9.68).

Expectations for education

The LA is legally responsible for securing the educational provision identified in Section F. The named education setting however will usually make the specified provision often supported by additional allocated LA high-needs funding. '*The headteacher or principal of the school, college or other institution named in the EHC plan should ensure that those teaching or working with the child or young person are aware of their needs and have arrangements in place to meet them*' (CoP, 9.130).

In practice, the SENCO, alongside teachers and TAs, should ensure that all involved in supporting the CYPn are made familiar with the EHC plan's contents and that all provision and resources specified are in place. Should the setting be unable to deliver what is specified, the LA has a duty to secure that provision from elsewhere. An example of this might include an LA commissioning specialist teaching, eg for a CYPn with severe dyslexia.

Expectations for health care

In Section G of the EHC plan, any health care provision stipulated remains the responsibility of the CCG/NHS England. It might reasonably include specialist support and therapies, eg medical treatments, delivery of medications, OT and physiotherapy, nursing support such as for epilepsy, use of feeding tubes and tracheostomies, specialist equipment, wheelchairs and continence supplies (CoP, 9.69).

The expectation stated clearly in the CoP (9.141) is that joint arrangements underpinning individual EHC plans include agreement about funding responsibilities and arrangements and thus requires the commissioning of agreed, specified services. CCGs must ensure clear lines of communication with the LA regarding health service commissioning to ensure health provision such as that listed above can be delivered in line with the statutory requirement.

Expectations for social care

Any social care provision specified in the EHC plan remains an ongoing responsibility as part of the existing duties of social care services. This includes the requirement to fulfil the duties as set out in the Children Act 1989 to meet the needs of disabled CnYP. Adult services will usually provide the care elements of a plan when YP are aged 18 and over (CoP, 9.138). The Care Act 2014 places a duty upon the LA to ensure a smooth transition into adult care services. For some YP the LA may deem it more appropriate for them to remain within children's services for as long as their EHC plan is in place, up to the age of 25. This flexibility should allow for change to be staggered across EHC provision (CoP, 9.137-9.139).

Provision: alternative arrangements

In implementing the EHC plan, the parent or YPn can make suitable alternative arrangements for special educational provision including elective home education or through the independent education sector. In these instances, the LA must be satisfied that the arrangements are suitable before being relieved of its duty to make provision (CoP, 9.133). This might include LA commissioners making a visit to the identified setting for quality assurance purposes. If the arrangements are deemed unsuitable, the LA either can name an identified appropriate educational setting or may choose to provide financial assistance to support access to alternative provision. There is, however, no obligation for the LA to meet the costs of these arrangements (CoP, 9.134).

Where the parent or YPn takes responsibility for securing suitable educational provision, the health commissioning body remains responsible for any health care written into the EHC plan. Should the parent or YPn make their own health care arrangements, the health commissioning body, just like the LA, must be satisfied that these measures are suitable. If those are judged to be unsatisfactory, the health commissioning body would either make the arrangements as specified originally in the EHC plan or support the parents or YPn to secure appropriate health care arrangements (CoP, 9.135).

This flexible approach is deliberately designed to enable parents or YP to secure alternative arrangements if such arrangements are considered to be most appropriate to meet the CYPn's particular SEN and circumstances (CoP, 9.131–9.136).

EHC plans in practice: research findings

One of the fundamental principles of the SEND CoP entails the greater choice and control offered to CnYP and parents regarding education, health and social care services. This, alongside close collaboration between all parties, was intended to provide high quality support and provision to meet the needs of CnYP with SEN. What the Code of Practice describes would seem challenging for all sectors to implement.

A DfE funded report (2016) presented findings from a small cohort of families with EHC plans using the Personal Outcomes Evaluation Tool (POET). Practitioners from education, health and social care contributed their perspectives. It is worth noting that the highest practitioner response came from those in education, with the majority of respondents being SENCOs. This response rate provides support for the perception that that responsibility lies primarily with education practitioners, with health and social care seen as lesser partners. Table 12.1 identifies some of the main findings from education, health and social care practitioner perspectives.

A later report (DfE, 2017c) surveyed the experiences of those CnYP and their parents who had EHC plans issued in the calendar year 2015. Almost three-quarters of those questioned for the survey agreed that their EHC plan led to the CYPn getting the help and

Table 12.1 *EHC practitioner evaluation of EHC plans*

Themes	Combined EHC practitioner responses
Collaboration between EHC practitioners	65% felt EHC plans aided practitioner collaboration
Removing barriers to learning	78% agreed EHC plans enabled CnYP to take part in school and learning
Preparing for the future	69% said EHC plans helped CnYP think about and plan for the future
Identifying and meeting needs	77% said EHC plans helped them understand CnYPs needs 73% saw EHC plans provide individually tailored support; 75% saw CnYP put at the heart of planning
70 LA responses from across England 2989 EHC practitioner responses in total	

support that they needed and over two-thirds agreed it had improved the CYPn's experience of education. Over half of the respondents were confident that the EHC plan would support community participation and independent living while just under half were confident about the EHC plan preparing YP to find work.

A DfE (2018b) investigation included assessment of the quality of EHC plans and identified the following three elements as necessary to create a high quality plan.

1.   Inclusion of all statutory requirements.

2.   Being accessible (particularly to YP and parents).

3.   Being representative of the underpinning principles of the CoP.

The second and third elements were found not to be as robustly addressed. It was identified that in order to be accessible, EHC plans benefited from being written in plain English and with CYPn and parent views written in the first person to make the content personal. Where the underpinning principles of the CoP were not addressed, there were a number of contributory factors including:

•   parent and CYPn voice not threading throughout the EHC plan;

•   a lack of balance between needs and capabilities;

•   a lack of clarity both in identifying contributors, collaborators and providers and regarding the timing, quantity and frequency of support required;

- a lack of future-focused outcomes including planned transitions;
- an absence of SMART outcomes broken down into measurable steps.

Local area SEND inspections

The local area comprises the LA, health commissioners and providers. SEND inspections were implemented in 2016 to inspect the effectiveness of local areas in fulfilling their duties in relation to the CoP. They are jointly conducted by Ofsted and the CQC. Three key areas are assessed.

1. Identifying CnYP's SEND.
2. Meeting the needs of CnYP who have SEND.
3. Improving outcomes for CnYP who have SEND.

Each inspection results in an outcomes letter being issued to the local area LA and health leaders, identifying strengths and areas to be addressed against the three aspects identified above. Where significant concerns are held, the local area is charged with providing a written statement of action (WSOA) identifying remediating work and associated timescales.

The Ofsted and CQC (2017) report identified emerging themes for the first 30 local area SEND inspections completed, concerning a high use of exclusion, poor access to therapy services and CAMHS, together with a lack of progress in implementing a co-ordinated 0 to 25 service across all services. Of particular note were flaws in the process for obtaining the statutory contributions from health and care practitioners as part of EHC assessments, resulting in EHC plans being of poor quality. Subsequent local area inspections have continued to identify that this is an ongoing concern.

CRITICAL QUESTIONS

Locate the written outcomes letter for your local area using the Ofsted Reports website and respond to the following questions: https://reports.ofsted.gov.uk/

- How do EHC plans feature in the three sections of the letter: identifying CnYP's SEND; meeting the needs of CnYP with SEND; and improving outcomes?

- How effectively do EHC providers co-ordinate their services from 0 to 25 for CnYP with SEND?

- In your practitioner role, what implications might there be for your practice?

Conclusion

This chapter examines how EHC plans are implemented and the implications for practice across services. We have identified that much of the research analysis and reporting is based on plans produced quite early under the new CoP. Whether EHC plans being implemented today are more effective remains to be seen, bearing in mind effectiveness may not necessarily be viewed in the same way by CnYP, their parents and practitioners in EHC.

Further reading and web-based materials

This is a qualitative study that explores SENCOs' perspectives of the EHC plan process and discusses three key themes.

Boesley, L and Crane, L (2018) *Forget the Health and Care and Just Call them Education Plans: SENCOs' Perspectives on Education, Health and Care Plans.* [online] Available at: onlinelibrary.wiley.com/doi/10.1111/1471-3802.12416 (accessed 9 August 2019).

This paper examines the academisation of schools as well as reasons why a decreasing percentage of pupils are considered to have SEN in academies.

Academisation of Schools in England and Placements of Pupils with Special Educational Needs: An Analysis of Trends, 2011–2017. [online] Available at: doi.org/10.3389/feduc.2019.00003 (accessed 9 August 2019).

13 The review process

The review process

- The annual review
  - Early review
  - Reassessment
  - Cease to maintain
- Transfer between LAs and CCGs
- Transport
- Resolving disagreements
  - The tribunal process
  - The role of the practitioner
  - Complaints procedures

This chapter provides:

- an exploration of the annual review process;
- an exploration of the implications for CnYP with an EHC plan who move between LAs;
- a discussion of the implications of transport arrangements;
- further discussion on how to resolve disagreements.

The annual review

Every EHC plan, once issued, must be reviewed formally on at least an annual basis (CoP, 9.116). Education settings may also choose to hold additional, informal reviews more regularly, ie termly. The purpose of the review is to monitor the progress made towards outcomes and longer-term aspirations and to determine whether they remain appropriate (CoP, 9.166). It **must** be undertaken in partnership with the CYPn and their parent (CoP, 9.168). This formal review provides the opportunity to undertake a holistic analysis of information held by parents, CnYP, and education, health and social care practitioners. It enables a consideration of matters such as changes to outcomes, provisions or types of education setting (CoP, 9.167). There may also be discussions held as to whether to discontinue the EHC plan.

As with the EHC assessment, there are statutory timescales to be met for the annual review process, described in detail in the SEND CoP (9.166–9.172). It is worth noting that the LA holds responsibility for adherence to all statutory timescales related to EHC plans. Addressing this complexity of timing and information processing requires LA SEN officers to be very familiar with Chapter 9 of the CoP.

Practitioners from health and social care **must** co-operate with the LA during reviews (CoP, 9.169) and a representative from health and social care **must** be invited to the annual review meeting (CoP, 9.176). However, our experience would indicate that attendance at the annual review meeting is predominantly by education practitioners and parents, unless the CYPn is looked after or has particularly complex SEN.

For CnYP who are looked after, it is advised that their EHC plan should not be reviewed in isolation but should be viewed alongside their CP and particularly their PEP. Yet as the CDC guidance (2016, p 4) identifies,

> *aligning the annual review of an EHC plan with a review of the child's care plan can be difficult because of the number of people involved, the timescales for the reviews and the nature of the care plan review meeting compared to the EHC annual review.*

The review process should enable the plan to be amended if necessary, so that it remains relevant to the CYPn's needs (CoP, 9.186). Changes can be minor or specific, the parents or CYPn must be involved, amendments must be clearly identified, and the amended plan issued.

Early review

Should a CYPn's SEN change or the education, health or care provision no longer meet the identified needs, the LA should hold a review as soon as possible (CoP, 9.130). In practice, this request to review early may be instigated by the parents/YP or the education setting. The review process remains the same. IPSEA (2019) advise that an early/emergency review may also be deemed appropriate for CnYP with an EHC plan who are at risk or who have been excluded.

Reassessment

A reassessment may be considered necessary if the CYPn's SEN change considerably (CoP, 9.186), eg as the result of a degenerative condition or when adult services need to identify what support is required. The LA can decline to reassess if it believes that the CYPn's needs have not altered significantly or if less than 6 months have passed since the last assessment was carried out (CoP, 9.187). The reassessment process follows the same process and timescale as an EHC assessment and parents/YP have the same rights to appeal (CoP, 9.191).

Cease to maintain

The LA can only cease to maintain an EHC plan for two reasons. Firstly, when it determines it is no longer necessary to be maintained because the CYPn no longer requires special educational provision and secondly, when it is no longer responsible for the CYPn (CoP, 9.199). For YP aged 19 and over the LA will need to be confident that the specified educational/training outcomes have been achieved. For those YP of compulsory school/participation age who have been excluded or become disengaged, every effort must be made by those practitioners involved and by the LA to re-engage them with training or education (CoP, 9.202). The EHC plan cannot be automatically ceased and may require amending if SEN provision is still required.

Transfer between LAs and CCGs

As already discussed in Chapter 6, the original LA has a statutory duty to transfer the EHC plan on the day of the move for children who move between LAs. Once transferred, the new LA becomes responsible for maintaining the plan and securing the special educational provision as described. If the named placement has to change, eg due to distance, either like-for-like provision must be made, or a temporary placement secured at an appropriate education setting until the EHC plan is formally amended through the annual review process or through reassessment. For CnYP moving out of England, the LA must send a copy of the EHC plan to the new LA/board, but the new LA/board is not obligated to maintain it.

CCGs hold the same responsibilities for notification and transferring health information about the EHC plan. If the new CCG finds it 'not practicable' to make the health provision described in the EHC plan, it **must** request the relevant LA to either review the plan or make a reassessment (CoP, 9.163).

Transport

While transport accounts for just four short paragraphs in the 2015 SEND CoP, in reality in our experience it gives rise to some of the most contentious conversations, as a quick search on the internet reveals. LA general transport arrangements and policies should be sited on the LO. Transport is not typically expected to be recorded in an EHC plan and the CoP indicates that this would be only for exceptional cases (CoP, 9.215). What has become reported on more frequently is that the rise in EHC plans alongside the increased use of educational placements in the independent special school sector are resulting in increasingly long journeys for CnYP and increasing costs for LAs (Weale, 2018).

Resolving disagreements

We have already discussed the importance of trying to resolve disagreements from an early stage and at a local level; however, sometimes this is not possible and a formal appeal can be lodged with SENDIST.

Chapter 11 of the SEND CoP, 'Resolving disagreements', identifies key principles and provides the reader with a helpful chart outlining avenues for complaints and redress for CnYP who have an EHC plan. Appeals to SENDIST could only be brought against educational aspects of a CYPn's educational provision. However, recent changes in April 2018 to the Children and Families Act 2014 have allowed a single route of redress enabling appeals to be brought not only on matters of educational need but against all aspects of an EHC plan. SENDIST will be able to make non-binding recommendations on health and social care aspects.

The tribunal process

Chapters 6 and 8 of this book have examined some of the routes for resolving disagreements. The formal process is by way of registering an appeal with SENDIST.

It is important to note that an appeal to SENDIST cannot be registered unless mediation has been considered. Despite this process the number of appeals to SENDIST has risen over the past few years as already discussed in Chapter 8.

A YP can register an appeal in their name if they are over compulsory school age and up until they reach the age of 25. Parents can also register an appeal for CnYP from birth to the end of compulsory schooling. These appeals can be made in the following areas after decisions have been made by the LA not to:

- carry out an EHC needs assessment;
- issue an EHC plan;
- amend the EHC plan after a review or reassessment;
- continue to maintain the EHC plan;

or about the

- description of the CYPn's needs;
- provision specified to meet those needs;
- educational placement.

An appeal **must** be registered within 2 months of the LA sending a notice to the parent or YP with regard to their decision. The tribunal powers with regard to what decisions it can make are governed by the Children and Families Act 2014. In essence, the tribunal can dismiss the appeal or order the LA to make amendments for each/any of the disputed points listed above.

The role of the practitioner

The tribunal process can be very stressful for all involved. Truss (2008) describes the '*cost in terms of time, effort and emotion incalculable*' (p 371), while Bennett (1998) identifies that the process polarises all concerned.

As a practitioner attending a tribunal you will be required to collect and present evidence. This may take a number of forms but will especially consist of details of the CYPn's needs, what provision is currently in place and what will be required in the future.

IMPLICATIONS FOR PRACTICE

Parents and professionals occupy different positions in relation to children. The parent has a much greater stake in the partnership than the professional

(Todd and Higgins, 1998, p 228)

You have been asked by both the LA and the CYPn's parents to attend a tribunal as a witness for them. Assuming the role of a practitioner you are familiar with and considering this quote, reflect on the following question.

- How would you ensure your evidence does not undermine either the parent or the LA?

Complaints procedures

While the SEND CoP discusses in detail the role of mediation and the process for appealing to SENDIST, it also describes other complaints procedures including those for health and social services (CoP, 11.67–11.111). Table 13.1 illustrates this.

Table 13.1 Complaints procedures

Institution/organisation	Process (ascending order)
Education 1. Nursey EYFS 2. Schools (state funded) 3. Academies, free schools, independent schools 4. Post-16 institutions 5. The LA	1. Manager in first instance, Ofsted 2. Institution complaints procedure, schools' complaints unit 3. Schools complaints procedure, panel (including one independent member), EFA (academies and free schools only), Secretary of State (independent schools) 4. Institution complaints procedure, principal, Skills Funding Agency or EFA 5. The Local Government Ombudsman (LGO)
Health care 1. Individual provision 2. Commissioned services	1. To the NHS provider, eg NHS Hospital Trust, Local Healthwatch, the Parliamentary and Health Service Ombudsman (PHSO) 2. CCG
Social care	LA complaints procedure by informing either the Director of Children's Services or the Designated Complaints Officer, the LGO

It is interesting to note that the number of routes available for complaints about educational aspects of the EHC plan far outweigh those for both health and social care combined, thus further adding to the perception that education has a more significant role in the EHC plan process.

Conclusion

Effective annual reviews held with a high level of participation from all practitioners involved ensure that the holistic understanding of the CYPn is maintained. Such reviews should support progress towards both the specified outcomes and longer-term aspirations. The DfE (2019d) EHC plan statistics however evidence the following:

* rising numbers of EHC plans;

* decreasing numbers of EHC plans completed within the statutory 20-week timescale;

* a corresponding rise in both formal and informal disagreements.

The EHC plan process appears, by necessity, to be focused on funding – who pays – and the limitations or absence of provision. This would seem a far cry from the original intentions of the new SEND CoP to be child-centred and needs-led.

Further reading and web-based materials

This article is written from the point of view of law and children's rights. It considers to what extent the Children and Families Act 2014 has enabled CnYP with SEND to realise agency and autonomy.

Harris, N and Davidge, G (2019) The Rights of Children and Young People under Special Educational Needs Legislation in England: An Inclusive Agenda? *International Journal of Inclusive Education*, 23(5): 491–506.

This research considers the role of EPs as expert witnesses in SENDIST hearings on behalf of the LA. It suggests EPs should support their LAs in managing the appeals process more effectively and that their role might be reconfigured so that mediation is at the heart of their work.

Yates, M and Hulusi, H (2018) Missed Opportunities: What Can Be Learnt from EPs' Experiences at SEN Tribunals? *Educational Psychology in Practice*, 34(3): 300–14.

References

Allan, J and Youdell, D (2017) Ghostings, Materialisation and Flows in Britain's Special Educational Needs Assemblage. *Discourse: Studies in the Cultural Politics of Education*, 38(1): 70–82.

Apprenticeships, Skills, Children and Learning Act 2009. [online] Available at: www.legislation.gov.uk/ukpga/2009/22/contents (accessed 24 November 2019).

BACCH and BACD (2014) Medical Advice for Education: Recommendations for Paediatricians. [online] Available at: www.bacch.org.uk/policy/documents/MedicalAdviceforEducation-RecforPaedsBACCHBACD23Sept2014.pdf (accessed 19 September 2019).

Bennett, P L (1998) Special Educational Needs Tribunals: An Overview for Educational Psychologists. *Educational Psychology in Practice*, 14(3): 203–8.

Blatchford, P, Bassett, P, Brown, P, Martin, C, Russell, A and Webster, R (2009) *Deployment and Impact of Support Staff Project*. Research Brief 148 DCSF. [online] Available at: maximisingtas.co.uk/assets/content/dissressum.pdf (accessed 2 September 2019).

Boesley, L and Crane, L (2018) Forget the Health and Care and Just Call Them Education Plans: SENCOs' Perspectives on Education, Health and Care Plans. *Journal of Special Educational Needs*, 18(51): 36–47.

Bolton, G (2010) *Reflective Practice: Writing and Professional Development*, 3rd edition. Los Angeles: Sage.

Boyle, D, Slay, J and Stephens, L (2010) *Public Services Inside Out: Putting Co-Production into Practice*. London: New Economics Foundation.

Broach, S, Clements, L and Read, J (2015) *Disabled Children: A Legal Handbook*, 2nd edition. London: Legal Action Group. Education and Service Trust Limited.

Bunn, J (2019) 'Warning over budget cuts as health visitor numbers plummet' *Nursing Times* 21 March. [online] Available at: www.nursingtimes.net/news/public-health/warning-over-budget-cuts-as-health-visitor-numbers-plummet-21-03-2019/ (accessed 16 September 2019).

Care Act 2014. [online] Available at: www.legislation.gov.uk/ukpga/2014/23/contents/enacted (accessed 19 September 2019).

CDC (2016) *The Role of Independent Reviewing Officers in Education, Health and Care Needs Assessments and Plans for Looked After Children and Young People with Special Educational Needs*. [online] Available at: councilfordisabledchildren.org.uk/sites/default/files/field/attachemnt/Role%20of%20the%20IRO.pdf (assessed 28 September 2019).

Children Act 1989. [online] Available at: www.legislation.gov.uk/ukpga/1989/41/contents (accessed 28 August 2019).

Children Act 2004. [online] Available at: www.legislation.gov.uk/ukpga/2004/31/contents (accessed 24 November 2019).

Children and Families Act 2014. [online] Available at: www.legislation.gov.uk/ukpga/2014/6/contents/enacted (accessed 28 August 2019).

Children and Young Persons Act 2008. [online] Available at: www.legislation.gov.uk/ukpga/2008/23/contents (accessed 24 November 2019).

Chronically Sick and Disabled Persons Act 1970. [online] Available at: www.legislation.gov.uk/ukpga/1970/44/contents (accessed 16 September 2019).

Contact (2017) Parent Carer Forums in 2017: How is Parent Carer Participation Working Across England? [online] Available at: contact.org.uk/media/1165159/contact_annual_report_2016-17.pdf (accessed 12 July 2019).

Data Protection Act 2018. [online] Available at: www.legislation.gov.uk/ukpga/2018/12/pdfs/ukpga_20180012_en.pdf (accessed 2 September 2019).

Davies, M and Beamish, W (2009) Transitions from School for Young Adults with Intellectual Disability: Parental Perspectives on 'Life as an Adjustment'. *Journal of Intellectual & Developmental Disability*, 34(3): 248–57.

Department for Children, Schools and Families (2008) *The Education (Special Educational Needs Co-ordinators) (England) (Amendment) Regulations 2009*. [online] Available at: www.legislation.gov.uk/uksi/2009/1387/made?view=plain (accessed 2 September 2019).

Department for Children, Schools and Families (2009) *Lamb Inquiry: Special Educational Needs and Parental Confidence*. Nottingham: DCSF.

Department of Education and Science (1978) *Warnock Committee Report*. London: HMSO.

DfE (1994) *Special Educational Needs Code of Practice*. [online] Available at: https://files.eric.ed.gov/fulltext/ED385033.pdf (accessed 21 November 2019).

DfE (2001) *Special Educational Needs Code of Practice*. [online] Available at: assets.publishing.service.gov.uk/government/uploads/system/uploads/attachment_data/file/273877/special_educational_needs_code_of_practice.pdf (accessed 21 November 2019).

DfE (2013) *Ensuring a Good Education for Children Who Cannot Attend School Because of Health Needs: Statutory Guidance*. [online] Available at: assets.publishing.service.gov.uk/government/uploads/system/uploads/attachment_data/file/269469/health_needs_guidance__-_revised_may_2013_final.pdf (accessed 14 July 2019).

DfE (2014a) *Further Education: Guide to the 0 to 25 SEND Code of Practice*. [online] Available at: assets.publishing.service.gov.uk/government/uploads/system/uploads/attachment_data/file/348883/Further_education__guide_to_the_0_to_25_SEND_code_of_practice.pdf (accessed 2 September 2019).

DfE (2014b) *Social Care: Guide to the 0 to 25 SEND Code of Practice*. [online] Available at: assets.publishing.service.gov.uk/government/uploads/system/uploads/attachment_data/file/348928/Social_care__guide_to_the_0_to_25_SEND_code_of_practice.pdf (accessed 2 September 2019).

DfE (2015) *Supporting Pupils at School with Medical Conditions: Statutory Guidance for Governing Bodies of Maintained Schools and Proprietors of Academies in England*. [online] Available at: assets.publishing.service.gov.uk/government/uploads/system/uploads/attachment_data/file/638267/supporting-pupils-at-school-with-medical-conditions.pdf (accessed 2 September 2019).

DfE (2016) *Report of the Use of Personal Outcomes Evaluation Tool (POET) for Children with Educational Health and Care Plans Spring 2016*. [online] Available at: www.in-control.org.uk/media/239850/national%20ehcp%20poet%20spring%202016.pdf (assessed 28 September 2019).

DfE (2017a) SEN Support: Research Evidence on Effective Approaches and Examples of Current Practice in Good and Outstanding Schools and Colleges. [online] Available at: www.sendgateway.org.uk/resources.sen-support-research-evidence-on-effective-approaches-and-examples-of-current-practice-in-good-and-outstanding-schools-and-colleges.html (accessed 2 September 2019).

DfE (2017b) *Performance – P Scale – Attainment Targets for Pupils With Special Educational Needs*. [online] Available at: assets.publishing.service.gov.uk/government/uploads/system/uploads/attachment_data/file/617033/Performance_-_P_Scale_-_attainment_targets_for_pupils_with_special_educational_needs_June_2017.pdf (accessed 2 September 2019).

DfE (2017c) *Education, Health and Care Plans: Parents and Young People Survey*. [online] Available at: assets.publishing.service.gov.uk/government/uploads/system/uploads/attachment_data/file/709743/Experiences_of_EHC_plans_-_A_survey_of_parents_and_young_people.pdf (accessed 16 September 2019).

DfE (2017d) *Statutory Framework for the Early Years Foundation Stage*. [online] Available at: www.foundationyears.org.uk/files/2017/03/EYFS_STATUTORY_FRAMEWORK_2017.pdf (accessed 2 September 2019).

DfE (2018a) *Special Educational Needs in England: January 2018*. [online] Available at: assets.publishing.service.gov.uk/government/uploads/system/uploads/attachment_data/file/729208/SEN_2018_Text.pdf (accessed 2 September 2019).

DfE (2018b) *Education, Health and Care Plans: A Qualitative Investigation into Service User Experiences of the Planning Process*. [online] Available at: assets.publishing.service.gov.uk/government/uploads/system/uploads/attachment_data/file/695100/Education_Health_and_Care_plans_-_a_qualitative_investigation.pdf (assessed 26 September 2019).

DfE (2018c) *Working Together to Safeguard Children: A Guide to Inter-Agency Working to Safeguard and Promote the Welfare of Children.* [online] Available at: assets.publishing.service.gov.uk/government/uploads/system/uploads/attachment_data/file/779401/Working_Together_to_Safeguard-Children.pdf (accessed 2 December 2019).

DfE (2019a) *Special Educational Needs in England: January 2019.* [online] Available at: assets.publishing.service.gov.uk/government/uploads/system/uploads/attachment_data/file/814244/SEN_2019_Text.docx.pdf (accessed 2 September 2019).

DfE (2019b) *Special Educational Needs: An Analysis and Summary of Data Sources.* London. [online] Available at: assets.publishing.service.gov.uk/government/uploads/system/uploads/attachment_data/file/804374/Special_educational_needs_May_19.pdf (accessed 2 September 2019).

DfE (2019c) *Tribunal Statistics Quarterly: January to March 2019 SEND Tribunal Tables: Statistics on the Appeal Rate to the SEND Tribunal.* [online] Available at: www.gov.uk/government/statistics/tribunal-statistics-quarterly-january-to-march-2019 (accessed 13 July 2019).

DfE (2019d) *Statements of SEN and EHC Plans: England, 2019.* [online] Available at: assets.publishing.service.gov.uk/government/uploads/system/uploads/attachment_data/file/805014/SEN2_2019_text.pdf (assessed 30 September 2019).

DfE and DH (2015) *Special Educational Needs and Disability Code of Practice: 0 to 25 Years.* [online] Available at: assets.publishing.service.gov.uk/government/uploads/system/uploads/attachment_data/file/398815/SEND_Code_of_Practice_January_2015.pdf (accessed 2 September 2019).

DfE and DH (2016) *0 to 25 SEND Code of Practice: A Guide for Health Professionals.* [online] Available at: assets.publishing.service.gov.uk/government/uploads/system/uploads/attachment_data/file/502913/Health_Professional_Guide_to_the_Send_Code_of_Practice.pdf (assessed 30 September 2019).

DfES (2001) *Inclusive Schooling: Children with Special Educational Needs.* [online] Available at: https://webarchive.nationalarchives.gov.uk/20130405061945/https://www.education.gov.uk/publications/eOrderingDownload/DfES-0774-2001.pdf (accessed 25 November 2019).

DH (2001) *Valuing People: A New Strategy for Learning Disability for the 21st Century.* [online] Available at: assets.publishing.service.gov.uk/government/uploads/system/uploads/attachment_data/file/250877/5086.pdf (accessed 16 September 2019).

DH (2010) *Personalisation through Person-Centred Planning.* London: Crown Copyright.

Disability Discrimination Act 1995. [online] Available at: www.legislation.gov.uk/ukpga/1995/50/contents (accessed 28 August 2019).

Education Act 1944. [online] Available at: www.legislation.gov.uk/ukpga/Geo6/7-8/31/enacted (accessed 28 August 2019).

Education Act 1981. [online] Available at: www.legislation.gov.uk/ukpga/1981/60/enacted (accessed 25 November 2019).

Education Act 1993. [online] Available at: www.legislation.gov.uk/ukpga/1993/35/contents/enacted (accessed 28 August 2019).

Education Act 1996. [online] Available at: www.legislation.gov.uk/ukpga/1996/56/contents (accessed 21 November 2019).

Equality Act 2010. [online] Available at: www.legislation.gov.uk/ukpga/2010/15/contents (accessed 28 August 2019).

Equality and Human Rights Commission (2019) *Public Sector Equality Duty.* [online] Available at: www.equalityhumanrights.com/en/advice-and-guidance/public-sector-equality-duty (accessed 16 September 2019).

Etymonline (2019) [online] Available at: www.etymonline.com/word/commission (accessed 2 September 2019).

Frank, A (2005) *The Renewal of Generosity: Illness, Medicine and How to Live.* Chicago: University of Chicago Press.

Frederickson, N and Cline, T (2015) *Special Educational Needs Inclusion and Diversity.* Maidenhead: Open University Press.

Frost, N (2005) *Professionalism, Partnership and Joined-Up Thinking.* Totnes: Research in Practice.

Garner, P (2009) *Special Educational Needs. The Key Concepts.* Abingdon: Routledge.

Gersch, S, Casale, C and Luck, C (1998) The Waltham Forest SEN Conciliation Service Approach to Reducing Tribunal Appeals. *Educational Psychology in Practice*, 14(1): 11–21.

Godson, R (2014) What Does the SEN Code of Practice Mean for Health Visitors and School Nurses? *Community Practitioner*, 87(10): 11–12.

Hall, D and Elliman, D (eds) (2003) *Health for All Children*, 4th edition. Oxford: Oxford University Press.

Hanson, J, Codina, G and Neary, S (2017) *Transition Programmes for Young Adults with SEND. What Works?* London: The Careers & Enterprise Company.

Hart, R (1992) *Children's Participation: From Tokenism to Citizenship*. Florence: UNICEF.

Health Act 2009. [online] Available at: www.legislation.gov.uk/ukpga/2009/21/contents (accessed 16 September 2019).

Health and Social Care Act 2012. [online] Available at: www.legislation.gov.uk/ukpga/2012/7/contents/enacted (accessed 24 November 2019).

Hodge, N and Runswick-Cole, K (2008) Problematising Parent–Professional Partnerships in Education. *Disability & Society*, 23(6): 637–47.

Hodkinson, A (2016) *Key Issues in Special Educational Needs and Inclusion*, 2nd edition. London: Sage.

Hodkinson, A and Burch, L (2019) The 2014 Special Educational Needs and Disability Code of Practice: Old Ideology into New Policy Contexts? *Journal of Education Policy*, 34(2): 155–73.

Hodkinson, A and Vickerman, P (2012) *Key Issues in Special Educational Needs and Inclusion.* London: Sage.

House of Commons (2019a) *Special Educational Needs and Disabilities: First Report of Session 2019–20.* [online] Available at: publications.parliament.uk/pa/cm201920/cmselect/cmeduc/20/20.pdf (Accessed 25 October 2019).

House of Commons (2019b) *A Ten-Year Plan for School and College Funding*. [online] Available at: publications.parliament.uk/pa/cm201719/cmselect/cmeduc/969/969.pdf (assessed 26 September 2019).

IPSEA (2019*) Asking for an Early Review of an EHC Plan*. [online] Available at: www.ipsea.org.uk/asking-for-an-early-review-of-an-ehc-plan (accessed 30 September 2019).

Jackson, J (1970) *Professions and Professionalization*. Cambridge: Cambridge University Press.

Ko, B (2015) Education Health and Care Plans: A New Scheme for Special Educational Needs and Disability Provisions in England From 2014. *Paediatrics and Child Health*, 25(10): 443–9.

Lamb, B (2015) Chapter 6. Accountability, the Local Offer and SEND Reform: A Cultural Revolution? *Journal of Research in Special Educational Needs*, 15(1): 70–5.

Lehane, T (2017) 'SEN's Completely Different Now': Critical Discourse Analysis of the Three 'Codes of Practice for Special Educational Needs' (1994, 2001, 2015). *Education Review*, 60(1): 51–67.

Lenehan, C (2017) *These are our children*. [online] Available at: https://assets.publishing.service.gov.uk/government/uploads/system/uploads/attachment_data/file/585376/Lenehan_Review_Report.pdf

Lexico (2019) [online] Available at: www.lexico.com/en/definition/commission (accessed 2 September 2019).

Lindsay, G (2018) Inclusive Education Theory and Practice: What Does This Mean For Paediatricians? *Paediatrics and Child Health*, 28(8): 368–73.

Local Government Association (2018) *Have We Reached a 'Tipping Point'? Trends in Spending for Children and Young People with SEND in England*. [online] Available at: //static1.squarespace.com/static/5ce55a5ad4c5c500016855ee/t/5d1cdad6b27e2700017ea7c9/1562172125505/LGA+HN+report+corrected+20.12.18.pdf (accessed 26 September 2019).

Long, R and Roberts, N (2019) *Special Educational Needs: Support in England Number 07020,* House of Commons Library. [online] Available at: file:///N:/TeachingMaterials/DSAcademics/dsjg4/Writing%20Julia%20Morris/September%20edits/Long%20and%20Roberts.pdf (accessed 16 September 2019).

Mason, M (2008) *Dear Parents...* Nottingham: Inclusive Solutions.

Mental Capacity Act Code of Practice 2007. [online] Available at: assets.publishing.service.gov.uk/government/uploads/system/uploads/attachment_data/file/497253/Mental-capacity-act-code-of-practice.pdf (accessed 2 December 2019).

Mental Deficiency Act 1913. [online] Available at: www.educationengland.org.uk/documents/acts/1913-mental-deficiency-act.pdf (accessed 21 November 2019).

Mitchell, D (2013) *What Really Works in Special and Inclusive Education: Using Evidence-Based Teaching Strategies*. Abingdon: Routledge.

Mittler, P (2000) *Working Towards Inclusive Education Social Contexts.* London: David Fulton.

NAHT (2018) *Empty Promises: The Crisis in Supporting Children with SEND*. [online] Available at: naht.org.uk/news-and-opinion/news/funding-news/empty-promises-the-crisis-in-supporting-children-with-send/ (accessed 26 September 2019).

Nasen (2014) *Transition: A Quick Guide to Supporting the Needs of Pupils and Their Families When Moving Between Educational Settings*. Tamworth: Nasen.

National Children's Bureau (2012) *The EYFS Progress Check at Age Two*. [online] Available at: www.foundationyears. org.uk/wp-content/uploads/2012/03/A-Know-How-Guide.pdf (accessed 28 November 2019).

National Health Service Act 2006. [online] Available at: www.legislation.gov.uk/ukpga/2006/41/contents (accessed 16 September 2019).

NHS England (2018a) *Quick Guide: Guidance for Health Services for Children and Young People with Special Educational Needs and Disability (SEND)*. [online] Available at: www.england.nhs.uk/wp-content/uploads/2018/ 07/send-health-services-children-young-people.pdf (accessed 28 August 2019).

NHS England (2018b) *Quick Guide: Commissioning for Transition to Adult Services for Young People with Special Educational Needs and Disability (SEND)*. [online] Available at: www.england.nhs.uk/wp-content/uploads/2018/ 07/send-quick-guide-commissioning-transition-adult-services.pdf (accessed 24 November 2019).

Ofsted (2018) Joint Local Area SEND Inspection in Brighton and Hove. [online] Available at: files.api.ofsted.gov.uk/ v1/file/50000234 (accessed 2 September 2019).

Ofsted and CQC (2017) *Local Area SEND Inspections: One Year On*. [online] Available at: assets.publishing.service. gov.uk/government/uploads/system/uploads/attachment_data/file/652694/local_area_SEND_inspections_ one__year__on.pdf (assessed 26 September 2019).

Oliver, M (2000) Profile. In Clough, B and Corbett, J (eds) *Theories of Inclusive Education: A Students' Guide* (p 112). London: Paul Chapman.

Riddell, S, Harris, N, Smith, E and Weedon, E (2009) Dispute Resolution in Additional and Special Educational Needs: Local Authority Perspectives. *Journal of Educational Policy*, 25(1): 55–71.

Robinson, D, Moore, N and Hooley, T (2018) Ensuring an Independent Future for Young People with Special Educational Needs and Disabilities (SEND): A Critical Examination of the Impact of Education, Health and Care Plans in England. *British Journal of Guidance & Counselling*, 46(4): 479–91.

Sales, N and Vincent, K (2018) Strengths and Limitations of the Education, Health and Care Plan Process from a Range of Professional and Family Perspectives. *British Journal of Special Education*, 45(1): 61–80.

Shier, H (2001) Pathways to Participation: Openings, Opportunities and Obligations. *Children & Society*, 15(2): 107–17.

Special Educational Needs and Disability Act 2001. [online] Available at: www.legislation.gov.uk/ukpga/2001/10/ contents (accessed 28 August 2019).

Specialist Schools and Academies Trust (2011) *The Complex Learning Difficulties and Disabilities Research Project: Developing Pathways to Personalised Learning*. [online] Available at: https://files.eric.ed.gov/fulltext/ ED525543.pdf (accessed 2 December 2019).

Standards and Testing Agency (2016) *The Rochford Review: Final Report. Review of Assessment for Pupils Working Below the Standard of National Curriculum Tests*. London: The Stationery Office.

Standards and Testing Agency (2018a) *Pre-Key Stage 1: Pupils Working Below the National Curriculum Assessment Standard. For Use from the 2018/19 Academic Year Onwards*. London: The Stationery Office.

Standards and Testing Agency (2018b) *Pre-Key Stage 2: Pupils Working Below the National Curriculum Assessment Standard. For Use from the 2018/19 Academic Year Onwards*. London: The Stationery Office.

Terzi, L (2005) Beyond the Dilemma of Difference: The Capability Approach to Disability and Special Educational Needs. *Journal of Philosophy Education*, 39(3): 443–59.

The Special Educational Needs and Disability Regulations 2014. [online] Available at: www.legislation.gov.uk/uksi/ 2014/1530/contents/made (accessed 28 August 2019).

Todd, E and Higgins, S (1998) Powerlessness in Professional and Parent Partnerships. *British Journal of Sociology of Education*, 19(2): 227–36.

Tomlinson, S (2012) The Irresistible Rise of the SEN Industry. *Oxford Review of Education*, 38(3): 267–86.

Truss, C (2008) Peter's Story: Reconceptualising the UK SEN System. *European Journal of Special Educational Needs*, 23(4): 365–77.

United Nations (1989) *Convention on the Rights of the Child*. [online] Available at: www.ohchr.org/EN/ ProfessionalInterest/Pages/CRC.aspx (accessed 28 August 2019).

Weale, S (2018) Councils Spent £160m on School Transport for Children with Special Needs – Survey. [online] Available at: www.theguardian.com/education/2018/nov/20/councils-spent-160m-on-school-transport-for-children-with-special-needs-survey (assessed 28 September 2019).

Webster, R, Blatchford, P and Russell, A (2013) Challenging and Changing How Schools Use Teaching Assistants: Findings from the Effective Deployment of Teaching Assistants Project. *School Leadership and Management*, 33(1): 78–96.

Wenger, E (1999) *Communities of Practice: Learning, Meaning, and Identity.* Cambridge: Cambridge University Press, 2005.

Wright, K, Stead, J, Ridell, S and Weedon, E (2011) Parental Experiences of Dealing with Disputes in Additional Support Needs in Scotland: Why Parents Are Not Engaging with Mediation. *International Journal of Inclusive Education*, 16(11): 1099–114.

Index